REHAB & GROW RICH

REHAB & GROW RICH

ADVENTURES OF A

RENEGADE REAL ESTATE INVESTOR

PAUL DAVEY

Published by Advantage, Charleston, South Carolina.
Member of Advantage Media Group.

ADVANTAGE is a registered trademark and the Advantage colophon is a trademark of Advantage Media Group, Inc.

Printed in the United States of America.

ISBN: 978-159932-391-6
LCCN: 2013939963

This publication is designed to provide accurate and authoritative information in regard to the subject matter covered. It is sold with the understanding that the publisher is not engaged in rendering legal, accounting, or other professional services. If legal advice or other expert assistance is required, the services of a competent professional person should be sought.

Advantage Media Group is proud to be a part of the Tree Neutral® program. Tree Neutral offsets the number of trees consumed in the production and printing of this book by taking proactive steps such as planting trees in direct proportion to the number of trees used to print books. To learn more about Tree Neutral, please visit www.treeneutral.com. To learn more about Advantage's commitment to being a responsible steward of the environment, please visit www.advantagefamily.com/green

Advantage Media Group is a publisher of business, self-improvement, and professional development books and online learning. We help entrepreneurs, business leaders, and professionals share their Stories, Passion, and Knowledge to help others Learn & Grow™. Do you have a manuscript or book idea that you would like us to consider for publishing? Please visit advantagefamily.com or call 1.866.775.1696.

This book is dedicated to my beautiful wife Lisa whose unwavering love, friendship and support has been a constant whether we've been IN or out of the money; and to our terrific girls Anne, Jessie and Jackie - The Circle of Trust.

Table of Contents

Introduction: *The Flooding at St. Patrick's Cathedral* 9

Chapter 1: *This Sucks* 19

Chapter 2: *Lies Do Not Become Us* 33

Chapter 3: *No Cell Phones, No Crying Babies* 39

Chapter 4: *Floggings Will Continue* 47

Chapter 5: *Check Points* 61

Chapter 6: *Make Sure You Salute* 75

Chapter 7: *Kicked in the Nuts, and Other Lessons to Remember* 91

Chapter 8: *Motorcycle in the Living Room* 107

Chapter 9: *40 Projects to Sandy Lane* 117

Conclusion: *What Hump?* 121

Bonus chapter: *Sample Investor Cover Letter* 125

Frequently Asked Questions 135

Recommended Reading 141

INCREDIBLE FREE OFFER

Whether you have purchased this book or received it as a gift, you can go to **RehabandGrowRich.com** and sign up for two free months of our Rehab and Grow Rich newsletter. The newsletter includes case studies, success stories, profiles, and an expert interview of the month with attorneys, hard money lenders, insurance brokers, and investors using a variety of strategies. You will also find a host of useful resources on our website, including our **A-Z Pricing Guide**, available as a free download, which details renovation costs.

We offer an at-home study course that includes six CDs and a 120-page course manual covering virtually everything that you would encounter in a renovation. Additionally, ongoing monthly telecoaching is available, as well as live on-site training with me in NY. Visit our website for more information.

The Flooding at St. Patrick's Cathedral

The leak turned into a gusher as I scrambled out of the hole in the street under the spires of St. Patrick's Cathedral. It wasn't one of my best moments.

I was 19 years old and working as a laborer for a Con Edison subcontractor. My job was to jackhammer the street to expose the steam pipes so that Con Ed's steam fitters could take care of whatever repairs and upgrades were needed. Those steam lines deliver a lot of the heat to buildings in New York City, and they need attention now and then.

On this particular day, I was working on the corner across from Rockefeller Center and the cathedral with a crabby old Irishman named Barney. I had dug down about five feet and was standing in the pit running a jackhammer because some of the pipes are encased in concrete.

"Use your pick and shovel there," Barney called to me, just before lunchtime. "You're getting close."

Usually, you would hear a ping from the jackhammer when you were getting close. The point of the jackhammer hits a metal warning plate about a foot away from the pipe. The plate helps to stop you from running the point of the jackhammer right into the pipe and piercing it. That's always something to be avoided.

But I was a teenager and knew everything, and I didn't like Barney. The metal plates are usually seven feet below the ground, so I felt at liberty to really lean into the jackhammer awhile longer. And I did. And suddenly water was spurting. I scrambled out of the hole, thinking I'd hit a steam line. I didn't want to get burned.

We grabbed the jackhammer's air hose and pulled it out of the pit, and the water leak turned into a gusher. I hadn't hit a steam line. I'd hit a water main, right in front of St. Pat's. The five-foot pit filled within seconds, and now the street was flooding.

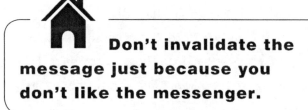

Don't invalidate the message just because you don't like the messenger.

Emergency crews came to close the street. They blocked off all traffic to the intersection, and rush hour was more than the usual mess. They closed the cathedral. Businesses shut down for the day. It took crews half a day to locate the shut-off. The story was on the TV news that night.

Somehow, to my amazement, I wasn't fired.

I've often thought about that Irishman who tried to warn me that day, twenty-seven years ago. Barney was a miserable guy, but he knew something that I didn't. He had experience. I didn't, but in my arrogance I closed my ears to him. I had little choice but to listen after I pierced that pipe—his brogue was thicker and hotter than ever.

I'm Irish Catholic myself. At age 16, I was ejected from a Catholic high school after tenth grade because of disciplinary and academic issues. And here I was, at 19, putting St. Patrick's Cathedral at risk of flooding. I was thinking lightning just might strike me any moment. My attitude has improved in the years since, and my wife and I have become benefactors of the St. Francis Breadline. Hopefully I've gotten a little credit with the Big Guy.

I think I learned something that day more valuable than a lot of what I heard in school. You have to be willing to take advice. You need to listen to people in the know, whether you like them or not. Your own arrogance can be your worst enemy. Don't ignore people with experience. Don't invalidate the message just because you don't like the messenger. I didn't want to hear what Barney had to say. He was telling me to proceed with caution. I found it easier to blast away. I was wrong. There are times to test the ground with a shovel and pick. Whether you are in a construction pit or at a foreclosure auction, that wisdom is golden.

It would be years before I would find myself applying that life lesson as a buyer of distressed properties, but I have thought about Barney many times since. I see his scowling face in those moments when I know I should listen up and proceed with caution. That's advice that would serve people well in many pursuits. It served me well in my years as a New York City cop, and it serves me well now as a real estate investor and rehabber.

THE BEFORE AND THE AFTER

At one point in my life, I wore a police uniform. I was a rookie police officer in 1987. I joined the New York City Police Department, and those were tough, long days. In my early days there, my take-home pay was about $63 a day or $315 a week. That was my compensation for standing in a place like the 40 Projects, which was one of the most violent housing projects in the city during the height of the crack wars.

Nobody in my family had been a police officer, but my mother, who is 83 now and grew up in Depression-era Boston, told me the only people who had houses back then were policemen and firemen. All the kids in my family were persuaded to take the police test when we were 16 or 17. My sister was a police officer for six months and after graduating from college became a schoolteacher. My brother was a policeman for about two years and then became a fireman and retired as a captain in the fire department. I stayed twenty years in the police; twenty-and-out was my plan.

When I was making plans to be more than an NYC policeman, I started Sligo Construction Corp.—a general contracting and building company on Long Island since 1987. I'm an active investor in distressed real estate through my investment company, B.A.T.M. Capital. I do several million dollars a year of distressed real estate investing for my own account in addition to listing and selling bank-owned properties, and I do over a million dollars in general contracting and building through the construction arm of my company.

This, then, is the story of how I went from a $5 per hour construction laborer and a New York cop to become a prosperous real estate investor and general contractor. I want to tell you about my experiences and share with you some things I learned along the way.

Some of these stories will make you laugh, some may make you gasp, and some will just leave you shaking your head. I once stood in the rain risking my life as a beat cop wanting something more. If you, too, have aspirations to get in out of the rain and do something more ambitious, I have information you need.

You wouldn't have picked up a book called *Rehab and Grow Rich* if you weren't curious about the prospects of buying distressed properties and making them better. What you do might involve repairing a fire-damaged house, or turning a small house into a colonial, or transforming a neglected house into the nicest one on the block.

Let me assure you: If you're smart about it, and if you pay attention to the lessons, you can certainly go far. You can transform properties and communities and make a great living in the process. You can go from $5 an hour to $250 an hour as a real estate entrepreneur, investing and developing. That's my story, and my strategy is growth.

When you are rehabbing, you're doing more than improving your own standard of living. My company can take the ugliest house on a block, a house that has been abandoned and abused, and fix it up, put a family in it, and get the property back on the tax rolls. Our efforts support not only ourselves but others in the housing and related industries—the contractors, real estate agents, insurance people and more.

You get the pure satisfaction of taking something that was neglected and making it beautiful and usable again. I have enough experience that I can visualize in advance the finished product, and everyone who stays in the business can get to that point. You can drive up to an ugly Cape and say to yourself, "This place is hideous and it only has two bedrooms and one bath, but when I'm done it will be a terrific center-hall Colonial with four bedrooms and two and a half baths." That is tremendously satisfying.

And it's highly profitable. I recently bought a Cape in Levittown for $220,000, and we began turning it into a center-hall Colonial. We immediately gutted the 1,100-square-foot first floor to the studs and cut the roof off it. At that point, the average person would have looked at it and shaken his head. But I knew that in four weeks it would be a Colonial with a roof, windows and siding, and the shell would be done. In six months I would sell it for $450,000 and it would be the best house on the block, where once it was the worst house. Neighbors love us, and new owners love us—hell, I love us!

Before (left) and after (right)

Levittown is a good community in Nassau County for turning properties around. At a recent closing, the buyers told me, "We looked at 63 properties. Yours was unbelievable because it was totally mint and fully renovated." I like making money, no question, and it's helping to pay my kids' college education, but words like that are great to hear. A young couple told me they had seen so many poor renovations and "when we saw this house there was no question we were buying it."

You're really helping the community by rehabbing, no question. You make money, but you also do a whole lot of good and get a lot of satisfaction out of it. To do well in this business, you have to have personal involvement. You don't have to be the carpenter, but you'd better at least go take a peek at your job and interact with the people who are doing the work there.

I love the transformations. Making money is nice, of course, but the construction business brings satisfaction even if you're not the guy or the girl with the hammer and nails. I show people the before and after pictures, and the results are amazing. I'm not doing the carpentry work these days, but I'm running the project and working with the architect. I have the vision.

IS THIS FOR YOU?

I'm looking to reach people who are excited about real estate. Perhaps you have a family member doing it, or maybe it was even a television program that turned you on to the possibilities. Maybe you are frustrated because you feel limited, either in education or finances, but I am here to show you that you can do it. I made it. I barely graduated from high school and started working at $5 an hour as a construction laborer. You can make it too.

I also have an affinity for contractors, because I am one. I'd like to see some of the people who are out renovating projects for wealthy real estate investors and developers get involved themselves in real estate as an investment. You'll see there's much more profit to be made as an owner than as the renovator. If you are both, all the better, and that's why if you have the rehab skills, you should start thinking about buying and selling houses.

> **In this book, I hope to reach the person looking to do more and earn more than he/she does today.**

Something that has always amazed me as a real estate broker is how few licensed real estate people participate in buying and selling houses, which is many times more profitable than the commissions that they make in selling real estate. The agents have access and get a first look at just about everything that comes out on the market. I hope to reach, them, too, with this book: Many are well-positioned to do far better for themselves. Sometimes it just takes a little push.

And finally, I hope this book offers some insight to potential investors. I've worked in my own business with private investors since almost the beginning. Today, I'm giving people the opportunity to become the "bank" much more often. Friends and family can write a first mortgage on one of my properties and get 10 percent interest just as if they were Bank of America. Today, when a CD is paying a 0.5 percent or 0.25 percent a year, to get 10 percent securely with me is a great opportunity.

I like to tell stories, and in this book you will see how I got started. You will learn about the importance of facing realities, and you will see some of those realities that you will face. I will demonstrate the need to play it smart and surround yourself with trustworthy people. If you are going to invest in distressed properties, I want you to know my insider secrets.

In each of these many stories, you will find some nugget of truth about the life I've chosen to pursue. This is a book about real people doing real stuff—some of it crazy, some of it smart—poking through vacant and dilapidated houses, bidding at auctions, even wading through sewage of one sort or another. It's not a book of step-by-step procedures. This book will include much practical advice, indeed, but it will do so in the context of life on the job.

CHAPTER 1

This Sucks

I t was raining again, a cold, late-winter downpour, and the gunshots echoed in the glare of the wet streets—just another night in the 103rd Precinct. And I was tired to the bone.

This was a quarter century ago, and I was a young NYPD cop assigned to a foot post in a violent housing project in South Jamaica called the 40 Projects. It was the 4 to 12 shift, and nothing was open, not even a place to use a restroom. It was utter misery.

On February 26, 1988, a police officer named Edward Byrne was assassinated as he sat in a police car. He was sitting in front of a drug witness' house in the precinct—the house of somebody who had seen a drug transaction go down—and four people who were connected to this drug dealer came up and executed him in the police car. (All four of those guys recently came up for parole and were denied, thank God—and I hope they never get out.)

Several blocks from the scene of that killing is where I had the privilege of working full time. Some of the killers lived in the 40 Projects. Thoughts of "I have to get off this corner" soon evolved into thoughts of "this cannot be the plan for my life." I was 20 years old. There were guys in the precinct at the time who were 50 or 55 years old, and I knew I didn't want to go that route, even if I could get off that dismal foot post.

GRINDING IT OUT

As I mentioned, I was already in the construction business at the time, so I was working two jobs doing concrete work during the day and working as a police officer. Both my jobs were hard work for low pay.

My wife and I managed to buy a house when I was 25. That was 1992. We used our savings to buy that $160,000 house, which stretched us. We had a beautiful little family growing, but I was back down to nothing after the down payment and repairs. I was grinding it out, frustrated, working seven days a week at one job or the other; and many days for 16 hours.

With some renovations, and with the rising tide of a strong housing market for years after that, the house gained plenty of equity. So I had sweat equity in a rising market, but I was still thinking small. By that time I was making $25 an hour in construction along with the small money from the police department.

But I didn't have a clear vision. I wasn't thinking big enough, and that's the mistake that most of us make. Most people who do amazing things are following a big plan or idea. We all have it within us to do that. *The Magic of Thinking Big*, by David Schwartz, spells out step by step how you can aspire to more, and it should be on the bookshelf of anyone who hopes to go far.

WORKING HARD BUT NOT SMART

In the construction business, I had been partners with my brother-in-law, and we usually had two part-time laborers. We each had our regular jobs, and four or five days a week from March into December as weather permitted, we were doing driveways or sidewalks and curbing. It was hard work for a small crew with one dump truck. I was truly grinding it out then.

I wanted to improve my situation. Even after five or six years as a police officer, the income was maybe $50,000 a year gross. I'd spent a lot of years in very hard and fairly low-paying work. For all of that work that my brother-in-law and I did in the concrete business, we made an extra $25,000 or $30,000 for nine months of hard labor. We were breaking concrete, finishing it, driving dump trucks, dumping, and it just wasn't time well spent.

I had the drive. I was willing to work 80-hour weeks. I did it for many, many years. I would work from 4 to 12 in the police department, get home at 1 in the morning, get up before 6, and get to a construction site by 7. Then, after a day's work, I'd go back to the police shift. I did it to provide a better situation for my family. But we were just getting by. I knew there must be something better.

Only a young man can do that kind of work, and I knew I couldn't go on forever that way. My grandfather was a carpenter who came from Ireland in his early 20s. He lived through the Depression and died at age 48. My uncle often used to say to me, "It's a young man's business." At age 18 it might be fun to swing a sledge, but it's no fun when you're 30 or older. Your body will wear out.

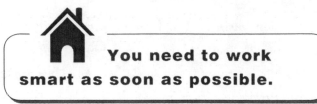

You need to work smart as soon as possible.

I credit myself with working hard, but I could have worked smarter much sooner. I'm glad I wised up when I did, and that's what I hope this book makes perfectly clear: You need to work smart as soon as possible. If I had kept grinding it out, nothing would have changed. The income would be no better, particularly considering inflation, and it might be a lot less these days. Actually, something would have changed: I'd be feeling a lot more aches and pains at 45.

HOW A CARJACKING LAUNCHED MY CAREER

In 1994, I was promoted to police sergeant and was working in the 83rd Precinct in Brooklyn. One day in late November two years later, I was riding into work with a friend, Bobby Grosso, also a sergeant. As we were on our way, four cops from our precinct witnessed a carjacking. Those were fairly common at the time: Somebody would come up to a car, stick a gun in the window, pull the driver out of the seat, and take off.

As the two RMPs chased the car, it crashed. Four guys bailed out, and the officers were able to grab three of them. Bobby and I, who were in his pickup truck, saw a fourth one running down the block, so we both jumped out and chased him down. But as I tackled him, I hit the curb and dislocated my shoulder. It could have turned out far worse: He had a gun in his waistband.

I was scheduled for surgery around Christmastime because my shoulder was in pretty bad shape. My shoulder injury, a torn rotator cuff, would put me out of the construction and concrete business for the spring season. I wouldn't be able to keep up.

As I look back, that injury was one of the biggest catalysts for change in my life. It forced me out of construction work temporarily while giving me a chance to pursue something that I was interested in—and I could do so without feeling guilty, which holds so many people back. I had felt the financial pressure of needing to support my family. When you have guaranteed income, it is hard to give it up. I would not have given up my construction income for the hope of making more money as a real estate investor—although the great thing about real estate investing is that you do not need to do it full time. There's no reason to quit your day job.

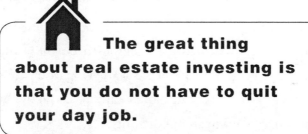

The great thing about real estate investing is that you do not have to quit your day job.

So I owe my career to a carjacker, in a way. The events of our lives are interconnected in ways we could never anticipate. In this book, I have plenty of advice on doing things the right way. But there are a lot better ways to get in the game than trying to catch a thief.

I had always been interested in real estate, and that's why I had bought a house by the time I was in my mid-20s. I had done a couple of renovations of distressed houses, and I aspired to make most of my money that way. Now was my chance. I would need recovery time and physical therapy. Time for me to get in the game.

I took the 40-hour course for my real estate license while I was still a cop and before I had the surgery that December. I applied to a local Century 21 office to work there part time right after the holidays. So about ten days after surgery, I began working.

AN IRRESISTIBLE OFFER

My office was in Massapequa, New York, not too far from where we lived. I was among the dozens of agents trying to get listings and show houses to people.

A couple months after I started, I saw a note on my desk one morning—and there was one on the desk of each of the 45 or 50 people working there. It was from the owner and manager of the office.

"Mark and I have been investing in some foreclosed properties and, having success with it, we're looking to do more of it. We're looking to see if people in the office want to participate with us." They were trying to attract additional capital, certainly, but it also seemed they were offering an opportunity.

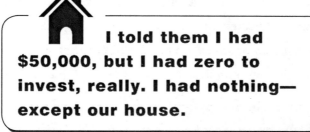

I told them I had $50,000, but I had zero to invest, really. I had nothing— except our house.

It seemed like what I had long been looking for. The owner and manager were offering all of us the chance to invest in distressed real estate with them and make some money—and they wanted to know who might be interested. They had a questionnaire asking how much we could invest and whether we had any skill sets that would be helpful. I was able to say that I had a dozen years of experience in the construction business, and I pointed out that I had a wealth of contacts in a variety of trades.

How much did I have to invest? I told them I had $50,000. That seemed like a good number, but I had zero to invest, really. I had nothing—except our house. In the five years since we had bought it 1992, it had gained enough in value that I was able to get a home equity line for that much, and a little more. I wasn't able to get the cash quickly enough for a deal right away, but I didn't want to say, "Yes. I want to invest with you guys and I have some construction skills, but I don't have any money."

Of all the people in the office who got that offer, I was the only one to step forward. I'm sure a number of them would have been in a position to say yes—but something held them back. I think people are afraid to try new things and to step outside their comfort zones. That office had some high-producing agents. They were making $150,000 and more in commission income, and that was sixteen years ago. They knew all about real estate. They may not have known the construction end, but they had been listing and selling properties for years and were knowledgeable and experienced.

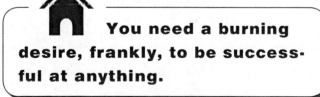

You need a burning desire, frankly, to be successful at anything.

Some of the agents in our office had worked with Mark and Rich for years. It was clear that they were living well, and the proof of their success was readily apparent in properties bought and sold. It's no secret if someone buys a property for $150,000 and sells it for $300,000. It's public record. You might not know how much went into renovations, but with that spread there's a good chance there was some profit there.

You need a burning desire, frankly, to be successful at anything. And money does matter. The more money you have, the better that life can become. You have access to all sorts of additional things. I'm forever grateful that I had that opportunity with those men. We went on to do millions of dollars' worth of deals together in the next decade.

In our first meeting, I told them I had a construction background and could put up $50,000. They had a deal they wanted to do the following week that would have required $40,000 apiece, but I couldn't set up the equity line soon enough for that. I would need thirty days. I explained that my money was tied up at the moment but I'd be in line for the next deal. So they bought a $120,000 house without me, and immediately resold it for $170,000 and made $25,000 apiece. Had I been able to join in, it would have been a nice $17,000 shot in the arm for me that was desperately needed.

About three weeks later, a deal came up in Islip, and this time I had the money. I became a one-third partner in the purchase. We bought the house at a foreclosure auction, and it was occupied. We introduced ourselves to the occupants and offered them relocation assistance, sometimes called "cash for keys," and they ultimately took $1,000 and left. One of the tenants was a hoarder, so we had quite a mess on our hands—I'll tell you about that adventure in Chapter

3—but the renovation actually went quickly, in six weeks, and we sold that house for a $64,000 profit. We each made $21,000 and change.

At the time, I was making around $50,000 for a whole year in the police department. It was almost half a year's salary in a six-week turnaround time. How cool was that? Instead of breaking my back in construction for $150 or $200 a day, I spent perhaps fifteen days at this house and made $21,000. That translated to about $1,500 a day, or seven to ten times my average earnings in the concrete business.

WHERE'S THE MONEY?

From there, we continued to do deals. These guys had a lot more capital than I did, but I wanted to be able to participate. For a year or two I ran up, at times, $100,000 in credit card debt. I'm not suggesting that would work for everybody. You have to find your own risk tolerance level. I was still running the construction at the time, so these guys were writing checks to my company to do their two-thirds of the renovation work. I was doing my third and I wasn't taking a profit on the construction and they weren't taking a profit on the brokering. When they went to list and sell house, there was no commission. If we purchased the house off the multiple listing, they weren't getting paid. That was our arrangement.

We would each go in for a third and nobody would profit other than on the sale at the end of the job, and we would chop up profits three ways. Through the capital they were giving me for the renovations, I was able to stay in the game with them even though I was charging much of the material that I was buying.

That meant I felt I had little choice at first other than to rack up my credit cards to buy cabinets and tiles and roofing and siding and sheetrock material. Nobody wants to pay 15 percent interest on those cards, but at the time I was making 25 to 30 percent profit a year with those guys. That made it work for me. I really wanted to change the situation I was in, and I could see the opportunities.

> **Most people figure they don't have the money to get started. But it's easy to attract capital from people who don't want to be hands-on involved.**

At the time I didn't think of raising private capital from other people. What stops most people from considering this business is that they figure they just don't have the money to get started. They lack the capital to make the buy. And that's what knocked me out of the running from age 20 to 30. Now, with more knowledge and experience, I realize that it's very easy to attract capital from people who have money but don't have the time or inclination to be hands-on involved in the project.

I didn't know that at the time. I did run up some credit card bills; these were easily covered by the income from my real estate deals. Then, when I got a comfortable amount of operating capital, I cleared all the credit cards. I haven't carried credit card debt for years, but it helped me to amass a nest egg so that I could swing ever-larger deals. Once you build up your capital, you can get a very good business going. We did.

In the real boom times, we were doing ten deals a year, starting a project almost every month. As soon as we cashed out, we would take those funds and either be buying at auction or buying off the multiple listing or from private sellers.

The capital was critical. If I had known in my early 20s what I know now, I would have attracted private capital and marketed to investors, offering a good rate of return. For many years now, I have worked with a small group of investors who will give me a mortgage for some of my projects much the way a bank would. I've established that I am an experienced, proven operator, so they will give me a first mortgage for, say, $200,000 at 10 percent, knowing I can renovate and resell the property for close to $400,000. It's a low-risk loan.

In raising capital, the first place for people to go is to friends and family. In today's market, so many people are retired with IRAs or 401(k)s or money in CDs that are getting 0.5 to 1 percent interest. If you can get them 8 to 10 percent in a safe vehicle, they will line up to do business with you. It took me awhile to get to that point. Today I have no difficulty in attracting private capital.

ACT BOLDLY...

I got in the game. I did what I had hoped for many years to do. Yes, I could have made much more money much sooner if I'd have spent half of those grueling 16-hour days raising private capital and forming relationships. I needed a bigger vision and access to better information. You can make much more money without working physically hard. My belief that I had to personally have the money to invest held me back. I didn't realize that you can leverage other people's money by partnering with them.

The bigger your vision, the bigger your results. The most successful men and women don't necessarily have more skills and intelligence than anyone else. What sets them apart is vision. People tend to discount their own skills, talents, and abilities and overinflate everybody else's. When you see someone who's doing something big, you think he has some magical powers that you don't have. The fact of the matter is, in almost every case, he doesn't. He just has a better vision and maybe a better plan and works on that all the time.

Once, I just thought day-to-day: "I need $1,500 this month to pay my mortgage and to make my car payment, and then I need an extra $400 for the child care," and so forth. I wasn't thinking, "Wow, how can I make $25,000 this month?" That's what you need to do. Then when you're making $25,000 a month, aim for $50,000, then $100,000.

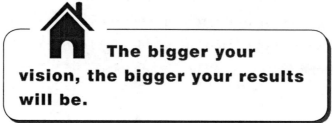

The bigger your vision, the bigger your results will be.

That big vision is what makes it happen. If you focus on why you can't do it, or what you don't have, and why people won't be interested in investing with you, you will slow yourself down. How do you see yourself? If you see yourself as a police officer making $50,000 a year, that's what you will be. If that's good for you, fine. If you want more, you can do it.

One of my favorite quotes is by the author Dorothea Brande: "Act boldly, and unseen forces will come to your aid." It's time to take those bold steps. Doors will open for you, and the things that you want will want you.

You need to get to know people. You need to network and get your name out there and establish a track record so that people see what you can do. That's what attracts money and people to you. It doesn't take a whole lot to get a track record. But you do need a couple of successful projects behind you.

Here on Long Island, we subscribe to a list service called the Long Island Profiles, which gives you dates and times and locations for all of the foreclosure auctions in Nassau and Suffolk counties. If you went to one today, you would find a dozen investors or hopeful investors looking to buy the properties. Most of these people are not in the construction business. Some are real estate brokers. Some are just people with capital, private investors. It's a great place to break in and hand out a business card.

If you lack money but want to manage projects and have something to bring to the table, you will find a ready group of people at those auctions. But in all the years that I've been going to them, I haven't seen anybody come up who's looking to do that. Nobody steps forward to say, "I'm looking to get involved, and I can run the projects or do such and such for you."

The best track record of all comes from working with a private investor for the first time and doing exactly what you say you will do. The investor gives you a $200,000 first mortgage, and when the property closes, you give the investor the $200,000 plus $20,000 in interest, which is 10 percent. The investor is delighted and will want to know when you are buying again and what else he or she can get involved with.

There's always a lot of money around, even today after the recession. Many people are investing their money poorly, at very low rates of return. If you have something solid to offer, and if you have proven yourself, they will be interested. You have to be of value to people. I offer investors a package and explain the mortgage terms clearly. I show comps of what renovated properties have sold for in the last three or four months. I present a reasonable expectation for a purchase and sales price, and I present my construction costs.

My profit is locked in at the time of purchase. There's no confusion for me. I'm not hoping that the market goes up or goes down. I know what this property will sell for in ninety days based on what's happening today in the market. I know my real estate costs and my construction costs. I have a profit analyzer and a construction cost estimator and can plug in the numbers within 3 to 5 percent for every job. We've done this for a long time.

Lies Do Not Become Us

I f you have seen the movie "The Princess Bride"—a favorite in our family—you may recognize the line, "We are men of action, lies do not become us." It may not be a pirate ship that you're striving to reach, but whatever your goal or wherever your destination, the lesson is a good one: Don't put up with nonsense along the way.

While channel surfing at a Maryland hotel, I watched an HGTV program on house flipping—that is, buying and reselling for a quick profit. The program featured a house in South Carolina: "Tom purchased this house for $100,000, and he put $20,000 into it. He has it for sale for $200,000." Flashing onto the screen, in big numbers, was "$80,000 profit."

Which was nonsense: The house hadn't sold yet. The ultimate sale price was unknown. No commission was factored in, or title insurance, homeowners' coverage, taxes—a lot of carrying costs that certainly would make that profit much smaller, even if the house were to sell for anything close to that projection. Most of us have been around the block enough times to know that a $200,000 for-sale sign doesn't mean a $200,000 sale—not lately, for sure. And yet people watch these programs and get excited. It's fantasy.

Nor do the TV fantasies reveal that manufacturers contribute free cabinets and granite and tile for the shows. That has a lot to do with how a $75,000 project can purportedly cost only $15,000. And the hosts aren't doing that work: It takes a dozen or more real carpenters and craftsmen to make it happen, and people tend not to work for nothing.

We want to know the real numbers. Lies do not become us. I know that house never brought an $80,000 profit. To honestly assess how you will do in this business, you need to see such claims for what they are: entertainment for the naïve. People do make profits, and nice ones—but give your expectations a reality check.

I have a friend who buys houses on Long Island. For a long time, he would say he made $100,000 on every house that he bought, but he wasn't good with math. He would say, "I bought it for $200,000 and put $40,000 into it, and I sold it for $300,000." Even if you counted that as $60,000 in profit—which it isn't because he's not factoring in all those costs, including his attorney fees—he is certainly not making anything close to what he claims. But you find that a lot: People exaggerate their successes.

Face it: You're not going to be piling up $100,000 profits. It happens, especially on bigger projects, but rarely with small ones. You can make money, for sure, with sweat equity as a homeowner, and you can make good money as an investor. I've been in this business for fifteen years. I've done a little over $19 million worth of distressed real estate transactions during that time. My average profit, per deal, is between 17 and 20 percent. You can get very rich on that kind of profit.

Congratulations if you hit one out of the ballpark—but don't expect it every time at bat. As the game goes, that's still pretty rare. Once, I made $137,000 on a total investment of $312,000. It was a 43 percent return on investment, and I was delighted. But I recognized that it was the exception. Even if you make 15 percent on deals in your self-directed IRA, your money will double every five years. At 20 percent, it doubles every four years. You can build up a lot of money in a short time, all while keeping your expectations reasonable. Self-directed IRA investing is a powerful vehicle.

Before (left) and after (right)

Those TV shows might motivate some people, perhaps, but they're soap opera. The real estate broker is carrying her dog around, and they're pretending that they're getting a renovation for a fraction of what it truly costs, and they're claiming big profits on houses that have yet to sell. None of that really happens. This is a real business with real numbers, and 17 to 20 percent, year in and year out, is a good profit.

"I CAN DO THAT!"

Such shows have raised expectations among 20-somethings who have developed champagne tastes with a beer wallet. My construction business has done government entitlement work and projects to assist first-time buyers, and the people sometimes feel they're going to get an HGTV-style kitchen with an oven in the center of the room and extreme ductwork and $30,000 cabinets. People's expectations have been dialed way up.

We did some work for a young woman in the first-time buyer program. She bought a house that needed to be renovated. We were going to put in a kitchen and a bathroom as part of the government's grant to help her get started.

"I'm going to gut the place to the studs, and then I'm going to sheetrock it," she told us.

"Who's going to do that?" I asked. (Uh, oh.)

"I'm going to do it. I've seen it on HGTV. And I'm going to take out this wall here between the kitchen and dining room."

She had no idea. This was her first house, and she had never done construction work. I knew that she was not qualified to do renovations, and certainly not to rip out load-bearing walls and install 150 boards of sheetrock and tape and spackle them. She had watched one or two episodes of the show and was convinced she could make major structural changes on a bearing wall. We wished her well, did our part of the work, and moved along.

You can applaud those TV fantasy shows insofar as they get people intrigued by the idea of fixing up a run-down or busted-up house. It's good to get excited, but don't linger too long in the afterglow. Demand real numbers. How much will the renovation cost, and for how much will the house really sell? If you are not a broker, make sure you're working with one who can show you the comparables of what has sold in your neighborhood in the last ninety days. That's what I mean by reality. That's how you can be sure you're not chasing some crazy price.

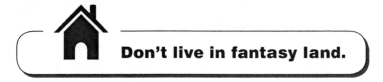

Don't live in fantasy land.

I list my homes for sale based on the prices of what's currently selling. I'm not in fantasy land. If houses are selling for around $300,000, I list mine for around $300,000. There's no point in listing it for around $350,000 because you're not going to fool people. You're not going to fool the market. Even if you get lucky and find somebody willing to wildly overpay, when the appraisals come in and that buyer tries to get a mortgage for the house, the bank won't lend the money.

It's a reality-based business, and real numbers are available for all of us, either directly to real estate agents and brokers, or indirectly to those who work with them. You can also look online. The data is not quite as accurate, but you can go to Zillow.com and get home values. I wouldn't invest that way because I want the real data of what's happening on the multiple listing, which to me is more accurate. However, there's enough to tell us where to price things once we figure out the rehab costs, and it can help us in making our purchase offers.

You'll note that I emphasized that we first need to figure out the construction needs and costs. You can't skip that part of the formula. You need to do it right, and you must know—or find out—how much the renovations cost. It's unlikely you can do it yourself. If you are in the business and have experience in construction and can do the work or know how to get it done, that's fine. You will understand the real costs, and you won't be kidding yourself.

But don't watch an episode or two of an HGTV show and think that you are equipped to install cabinets and tile backsplash and to re-sheetrock houses and change structural walls. Your time is valuable, so use it wisely. If you spend hundreds of hours doing a subpar renovation, you will hurt the resale value of the house. If you're an investor, your time is better spent searching for new deals and attracting private investors. I don't do my own work on projects now, despite my years of hands-on experience, and I don't recommend that people do that. Once you get rolling, the smart money is in locating good properties and lining up investors. If you're crawling under sinks or spreading spackle, you're saving a pittance by comparison to what you could be making.

CHAPTER 3

No Cell Phones,
No Crying Babies

I n the fishing mecca of Montauk, out at the tip of Long Island's South Fork, there's a bar called The Dock that's a great place to hang out after reeling in the striped bass and blackfish. Every fall, I usually take all the guys who work for me out for a fishing excursion to Block Island and environs. When we come back, we always stop at The Dock and have a couple of drinks. It's right on the wharf, a few hundred feet from the fishing boats, and you'll find a lot of the commercial fishermen there. It's a rough-and-tumble kind of place.

George, who runs The Dock, will throw you out if he finds you using a cell phone. I once saw him show a guy the door for tossing a drink coaster. Last time I was there, I saw a photo of a makeshift boxing ring. About thirty years ago, he used to challenge people to step into the ring with him. I asked him when and why he'd set up the ring—did he have somebody in mind? No, he said, it was open to all comers. He's one of a kind.

"No cell phones, no crying babies," a sign at the bar says. George means it. And you'll find that it's a good philosophy in the business of buying and selling distressed properties. Sure, you'll want a cell phone—just don't whip it out at George's place. But if you're going to be a crying baby, you might as well head for the door before you get ejected.

KNOW YOUR NUMBERS

Above all, in this business, you need to know your numbers upfront. It's too late to cry for help after you make a purchase—you need to calculate in advance whether it's a wise purchase. You have to know if the project is going to work for you, and if it doesn't work you can't get involved.

You need to make a cold, systematic business decision. Don't fall for the "wow" factor. Leave the emotions out of it. Whether you or someone else would just love to live in that house isn't going to help your bottom line if the numbers don't work. Knowing whether they work comes from due diligence and a basic set of formulas.

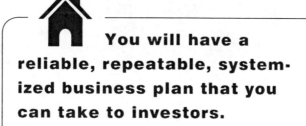

You will have a reliable, repeatable, system-ized business plan that you can take to investors.

See bonus chapter

When we buy, we know almost exactly what the profit will be on the way out—within 3 to 5 percent, and sometimes less than that. I can show everybody how to do that. It's a simple formula, and if you follow it without deviating and getting emotional and if you remain practical, you can do really well in this business.

You will have a reliable, repeatable, systemized business plan that you can take to investors. You can say: "This is our profit, this is how we make it, this is how we do our calculations—and if you look at our last six deals, you can see that we are close to the projection each and every time." You can invest with confidence. You won't be on a goose chase, wondering in six months, when the property sells, whether you made a profit, broke even, or lost $20,000. You will know before you buy—there's no rolling of the dice.

We use a pricing guide that tells us the going cost of whatever we need for a rehab project. On our "Rehab and Grow Rich" website, you can download, at no cost, the latest A-to-Z Pricing Guide. It will show you what we pay for every aspect of a renovation.

You have to inspect the property as closely as possible and know the costs you face. Once you have done enough projects, you will see that those costs are standard. You can look them up on the price guide and plug them into your calculations when deciding whether to make a purchase. For example, you know a 5-by-7-foot bathroom will cost you about $7,500 for a mid-range project. That takes out the guesswork.

Whether you're doing a kitchen or bathroom or installing electrical service or a heating system, with slight variations every house in America has the same components. Once you have a pricing guide for those components and once you have a relationship with the contractors, you can know the numbers for any job. If a house has four bathrooms and each needs to be renovated, you multiply your bathroom cost times four. Meanwhile, you are expanding your network of trusted contractors.

The multiple listing provides a wealth of information, beyond just sales prices. You can see how many days a property has been on the market, and how long on average it has taken other properties to sell. When I'm buying, I always look at both the sales prices of similar homes and their average time on the market. If ten houses have sold recently, for example, I look at both the "how much" and the "how long" and figure the averages. You need to be realistic about both so that you know what to expect.

If I'm looking at a three-bedroom, two-bathroom ranch in Medford, New York, I want to know what such houses have been selling for in Medford and how quickly they have been moving on the market. That information is available to us on the multiple listing. Usually, I can even go online and see what those houses look like and how they compare to what I'm thinking about buying. That gives me a good idea of the sales price after the property is renovated. Then I use our formula to compute the construction costs, figure in expected holding costs, and work backward from there to factor in the expected profit. That's how we come up with the offer that I will make.

It's a fairly simple formula for every property that I buy. If I buy six houses this year, I'm following the same formula each and every time. Once you get comfortable with the basic math and the few things you have to look for, the process becomes systematized. You're not reinventing the wheel every time you want to go out and look for a property. Because I go strictly by the numbers, at the end of the day it's very easy for me to decide—once I estimate the sales price, carrying costs, and construction costs, and figure in my profit. Not much is variable.

My projections are conservative, so my profits often are on the high side, but I don't count on that. I don't tell myself, "I sure hope the real estate market jumps 10 percent in the spring." If that happens, consider it a bonus, but that's no way to invest in real estate. Don't listen to some guru who predicts that the market will boom next year. We're buying based on what the market is telling us today. Real data, current information, not fantasies and hopes.

If the numbers clearly don't work and yet you still are pondering whether to buy the property, you're sinking into your emotions. You're not proceeding with a clear head—and that can wreck your bottom line. People let their emotions guide them when shopping for the house that they plan to live in themselves. They shouldn't, but they do. But when you're purchasing a property as an invest-ment—whether you will be renovating and selling it, or renting it out—the decision has to be free of emotion. Plug in the numbers, and they either will work or they will not, and there's your answer. If the formula says forget it, then that beautiful wraparound porch doesn't matter.

Dan Kennedy, in his book *No B.S. Ruthless Management of People and Profits*, drives home the importance of going by the numbers. He is a marketing expert, and the information in this book is invaluable. You need to know what your numbers are, and what they should be, and you must make it your business to make them work.

I recently had a vinyl siding job done on a distressed property. I pay my siding company $80 per square for twenty squares, the bill is supposed to be $1,600. It's tried and true. We've established it. This is the price. The siding guy asked me for $2,000. The math told me that was $400 too much. I knew he'd used twenty squares because I'd purchased the material, and $80 per square is what other contractors would charge. It was the going price that he had agreed upon, and so that's what he was going to get. I was ruthless—not as in mean, but as in adamant about going with the numbers.

I like that contractor, and I'll use him again. The point is this: In this business, people will try you all the time. When you get a bill for a service that doesn't jibe with the price you agreed upon, you have to challenge that. You can do so nicely, and the contractor may have his reasons for wanting more. But this one didn't have a reason. He just wanted more. I reminded him how much volume we send his way, and he agreed to the lower price.

WORKING AS A TEAM

It's not a hands-off business totally. You have to know enough to know whether a contractor is treating you fairly. As I mentioned, my A-Z pricing guide can help you get a handle on what things cost. It can tell you what reasonable costs are in New York, and from those figures you can get an idea for prices in most other areas of the country. It tells you what you should be paying for a roof and what you should be paying for hardwood flooring, and so on.

For those who don't have the personal knowledge of how a heating system works, or electrical, or plumbing, you can team up with other people who do, and that strengthens you all the more. That's how I got started. My partners, Rich and Mark, were real estate brokers. They had a lot more money than I did, and they knew a lot about real estate. But they had no knowledge of construction and had been getting hammered in pricing because they were pulling up in their Mercedes and wearing $3,000 suits.

> **I drove an old pickup truck and wore work clothes. I was one of the boys, and those guys weren't—so I was the partner they needed.**

What I brought to the team was a lot of knowledge about the construction business and a lot of contacts. I could talk to contractors as one of them. I drove an old pickup truck and wore work clothes. I was one of the boys, and those guys weren't—so I was the partner they needed.

CHAPTER 4

Floggings Will Continue

Ever feel like staring—like Hector Elizondo in "Nothing in Common" with Tom Hanks? Well, that's what it was. Staring. I turned to see this woman with a horrified look on her face. Everything seemed to be going all right, or so I thought. It took me a minute to realize the cause of her dismay.

I was wearing a shirt advertising Bert's Bar & Grill, a place I like to visit in the tiny fishing town of Matlacha, Florida. On the back of the shirt are these words: "The floggings will continue until morale improves."

Now, that might not be the best policy for managing a work crew, under most circumstances, but it does sort of sum up what I'd like to point out. You need to have people skills and the ability to run a quality construction crew. If you're going to get into this business, things can get crazy. And not only that, people can get crazy. Expect it, and maybe just go with the flow. You'll be smiling soon enough, when the money rolls in. And you'll have plenty of stories to tell. I know I do.

MAS RODENTOS

The first house that I bought with my partners Rich and Mark—the one in which I used my $50,000 home equity line—was a horror. We had bought the house at an auction, and we had only seen it from the outside. It turned out that the tenant had been a hoarder. He had left piles of newspapers and garbage, floor to ceiling.

We sent two laborers into the house to begin cleaning and hauling out the trash. They immediately came running out, yelling, "Mas rodentos." The property was overrun with mice. He'd kept dogs in the house in cages. It reeked of dog feces and urine, and the laborers needed to use ice picks to scrape the crap off the floor. We sealed the walls, floors and ceilings with a primer-sealer to lock in the smell, and I put mothballs in the attic.

The first few days were the worst, and I was starting to lose confidence. I worried that nobody would want to buy that house. The smell had permeated the hardwood floors. I wasn't sure if ice picks, mothballs and prayer would be enough to get the stench out. I had found a janitorial supply place that sells a $30 chemical that neutralizes any odor.

It was one of the worst messes I've seen to date, and I've been in a lot of houses. We got rid of the stench, whitewashed and carpeted the floors, put in a new bathroom, and did other extensive renovations—and managed a nice profit. I was on my way, with a new confidence that I could work problems out. But … phew!

Because we had bought the house at a bargain price, we did well despite those conditions. Those first few smelly days were unnerving—particularly because this was my first investment. I have learned there are always surprises when you're buying distressed homes, so expect them, but there's a lot you can do to turn a profit if you use common sense and think matters through. You may have moments of panic, but there are solutions. You need to follow a proven system.

Today, the worse the conditions that I find, the better I can do. A fire may have burned off a roof, or a tree may have smashed through a porch, but that also means fewer people will be interested in dealing with the property. That means I get it, and I get it cheaper, and I can turn a bigger profit—that is, if the numbers indicate it's worth buying. I know the numbers. I have my system.

I must say it's unusual to find yourself scraping dog crap off the floor with an ice pick. That's not going to happen in most normal situations, but even if it happens you can work it out.

WHEN THE CEILING COLLAPSES

"It was probably the worst day in the history of Sligo Construction to date," I told a friend about another unfortunate event that further illustrates how crazy things can get. It was many years ago, when we were working for Home Depot Expo, which did high-end kitchens and bathrooms.

We were doing a second-floor bathroom in a $1.5 million home in Locust Valley, a wealthy community, for an older couple. They had decided to remodel it and put it back in use. The husband showed me his office, and pictures of him with President George Bush Sr. The man was prominent in Republican circles and clearly wealthy. Their house was beautiful.

The Home Expo project manager asked us to start early because the couple wanted to get the project rolling. I went out with a couple of laborers to begin gutting the bathroom on a Saturday. They shut off the main water valve to the house and began to work.

As they were removing a wall sink, a pipe broke—and water began shooting out from the plaster as if from a fire hose. The shutoff valve obviously had failed, and the plaster was about two inches thick, so we couldn't get to the pipe.

The men had a couple of big 55-gallon trash containers in the bathroom, so they scrambled for them and did their best to catch the flow and dump the water into the shower stall. Little did we know, the reason the couple hadn't used that bathroom in years was that the shower stall leaked. The husband was away that day, and the wife didn't know where the outside water shut-off was. The bucket brigade to the shower stall went on for ten or fifteen minutes until I was able to locate the valve at the street and stem the flow.

Relieved to have resolved the crisis, I walked through the living room on the first floor, directly under the bathroom. I looked up and could see telltale signs of water dripping through the ceiling. In the old days, plaster was hand-troweled thickly over wire mesh. That meant a lot of weight lay over our heads. Only a few drops were forming, but obviously there was water in the space between the living room ceiling and the bathroom floor.

As I walked out of the room, I heard it: "Ba-boom!" I turned to see that a six-by-six-foot section of ceiling plaster had collapsed into the living room. It had demolished a table, sending a laptop flying and splattering all over an expensive Persian rug. The ceiling had exploded like a bomb as the weight of the water broke through the mesh.

I marshaled the laborers downstairs, and we began cleaning up the mess. The woman of the house, who was about 80 and a proper lady, came into the room as we worked and announced: "This can't happen. I can't have this. I have a dinner party here this evening."

"Ma'am, I'm sorry to say," I told her, "but when the ceiling collapses, your dinner party is canceled."

Moral of the story: Once in a while in life, the ceiling is going to collapse. It might be a plaster one. Or it might be a deal you had counted on. Maybe a project's costs will be considerably higher than you anticipated. Your best plans just aren't going to happen. The dinner party is canceled.

We did make things right with that couple. We replastered the ceiling and cleaned up thoroughly, even if it took quite a bit longer than the few hours before her party was to start. It wasn't our fault that the shutoff system had failed, but we split the cost of the damages.

I've been a contractor for a quarter of a century, so I have assorted horror stories, but that's still one of the best. My friend, to this day, sometimes sends me a text: "Possibly the worst day in the history of Sligo Construction." We both know what it means.

EXPECT SOME ROUGH PATCHES

That kind of stuff will happen. In the big scheme of things, it wasn't so bad. Nobody was hurt, and it didn't cost that much to take care of the problem. Today, I can laugh as I tell the story.

I don't laugh, though, as I think about those days standing in the rain in the 40 Projects as a young cop. I don't look back fondly at that time. It felt like a dead end, not a beginning and an adventure. Sure, I had some good times in the police, and it got better over time. I had the opportunity to be in organized crime units and made sergeant, but the early days really sucked. I don't get texts from friends joking about those days.

I saw the potential long ago for a better way. I have three daughters. Whatever they pursue for their careers, I hope that they will also be actively involved in buying distressed real estate, whether

> ### Today's problems are just part of your learning curve.

they do it with me or on their own. It could be a lucrative career. It's certainly a great way to grow your retirement income. I want that for them, and for their own children. I started slowly. I want them to get a fast start out the gate.

You have to keep moving forward. Even back in my days of grinding it out, I kept going and kept dreaming, and that's what leads to success. You have to be thinking of what's next and how you can do more and bigger things. Never let frustrations quell your ambitions. There will be bumps in the road, and you'll get knocked down. A ceiling will collapse here and there, but just get up and dust yourself off.

Back when I worked those 16-hour days and then would get a hostile phone call from some unreasonable customer, my wife would feel so bad for me. "I can take the beatings," I'd tell her, and it was true. I was after something better. I had a vision and knew I was moving forward. That's how morale improves. You keep your eye on the brighter days ahead. Today's problems are just part of your learning curve.

DEFUSING THE SITUATION

One time when I was a rookie police officer, I was called to a family dispute on the fourth floor of a low-rise housing project. Responding along with me was another rookie, a female officer. It was a terrible place with dark, narrow hallways. It felt like a cave. We knocked on the door, and a woman came out.

"It's my son," she told us. "I want him to leave." Behind her, the son appeared in the doorway. He was enormous, about 6-foot-8 and well over 300 pounds. He looked as if he could have killed both of us in seconds, and he was a bit agitated.

"What happened?" I asked.

"Nothing," his mother said. "I just want him to leave."

"And you?" I looked at the man.

"Right. I just want to leave," he said, and moved toward the door.

"Stop!" my fellow officer ordered. "You're not going anywhere." She put a hand on his chest. She was about 5 feet tall and a hundred pounds. Like me, she was new to the job, and maybe she thought she was taking a page from a police academy textbook. Or maybe she'd watched too many cop shows on TV. But as far as I could tell, nobody had been assaulted.

"Yeah? Why not?" the man growled at her. He was getting hot, and I wondered if maybe an assault was yet to come. He could have picked her up and thrown her down the hallway like a projectile. "I just want to get out of here," he repeated.

"Listen," I told the other officer, "I'm going to talk to this gentleman in the hallway here, while you talk to his mom inside the apartment for a couple of minutes."

He told me he had just been released from prison and didn't want a parole violation, and I agreed he didn't deserve that. Nothing had happened. He and his mother had simply argued. He had committed no crime. Neither of them wanted to make any complaint. It made sense to let him go, which I was glad to do.

I pulled my fellow officer aside and said, "We don't even need to take a report. Nothing has happened here." But moments earlier, she had been pushing his chest. I could see his temper rising. He might have exploded if she had continued that approach.

The situation didn't call for that, and I was able to defuse it. Don't escalate situations. Police officers never know what they might face, of course, and when people do turn violent and foam at the mouth, the officers have to call for backup, and out come the pepper mace and nightsticks. The officers do what they must. But sometimes, people who are new to an endeavor, whether they are cops or investors, get too aggressive when it's unnecessary. They get wound up, and they wind up others.

A lot of times you can defuse situations just by the way you talk with people and how you handle yourself. When you are renovating properties, things won't always go well. But people tend to make mountains out of molehills. If there's a little problem with a subcontractor, or an installation hasn't been done 100 percent to your satisfaction, there is no reason to go ballistic over it. You just address it. You call the workers back to make it right. Things like that happen, so don't blow it out of proportion.

Building inspectors won't be foaming at the mouth, ordinarily, but you'll find them coming in with bad attitudes. Maybe it was a fight with the wife, or a traffic jam. They may look to find problems. I've had guys want to reinspect what they've already inspected, even though I have the previous results on paper. One inspector wanted me to pull the roof shingles off a building so he could check the strapping. I keep copies of all documents and photos in a folder at home and in my car, so I was able to quickly show the inspection report, but if the inspector decides to come out for multiple visits, there's not much you can do. If you annoy them, they can bury your folders or order extra work. Instead of getting approved in two or three weeks, you can wait eight or ten weeks, or forever.

Most often, things go well for me; I can make a phone call and the inspector will ask that I just take some photographs to validate the work. They know the quality of what we do, and I have developed an excellent reputation. But calmness and politeness cost you nothing, and they go a long way to defusing troublesome situations before they even arise.

TWO-BY-FOURS THROUGH THE WINDOW

I bought a house in North Amityville, a pretty rough area, and when we were a few days into the renovations, putting in windows and doing some inside framing, a local tough guy stopped by and arrogantly told us that he was going to take a look around. He claimed his father or his uncle owned the house.

No, he wasn't going to come in, I told him. I explained that we were working and he wasn't covered by my insurance, and he left angrily. He'd chosen the wrong crew to try to intimidate. At the time, the guys working with me were mostly cops—wearing construction clothes, yes, but all carrying. He had zero chance of getting inside.

We foolishly left some lumber outside that night, and the next morning three two-by-fours had been smashed through three new windows that we had put in. It was pretty clear to me what had happened. I haven't had too many such incidents. But don't forget to put things away: In a tough neighborhood, particularly, you don't want anything that could be used as a projectile to be left lying outside overnight. When people are angry, whether at you or at the world, they tend to express themselves with whatever is at hand.

You could easily begin to feel overwhelmed when ceilings collapse or the unexpected comes along, but keep marching. In any endeavor, there are good days and bad. You will encounter these little problems—and they are indeed little when compared to the big promise that such investments hold for you and your family. Sure, they don't seem like little problems at the time. People can be infuriating. You shouldn't take it personally—but you don't need to tolerate bullies, either.

> **You will encounter these little problems—and they are indeed little when compared to the big promise that real estate investments hold for you and your family.**

My partners and I bought another house in Seaford that was a probate sale—which is another way to find good properties. The house hadn't been updated in fifty years and needed to be thoroughly renovated. It had a major termite problem, or so the owners thought: They had a $17,000 estimate from a termite company to rebuild a couple of walls. They lived out of state and had inherited the house when their mother died. They wanted a quick sale, and we got a good deal.

Another probate before (left) and after (right)

The first day we were there, a neighbor came over—one of those loudmouths who feel they know everything. He said he was a union carpenter who was out of work on disability with a bad back and asked permission to load some trash into the 30-yard container that we had brought into the driveway for the renovations. I try to be nice to people, especially the neighbors, so sure: If he had $100 worth of stuff that he wanted to pile in there, no problem.

He came back a few days later. He needed six two-by-fours, and could we spare them? It seemed a small request, so I agreed. Then he offered his services as a master carpenter, despite his bad back, for $200 a day, if we could pay him in cash, of course. No way would I do that, but we did go out of our way to let him put trash in our container and use a few pieces of our materials.

The sellers had been worried about a dormer that had been added years earlier without a certificate of occupancy. Along with the termite issue, that was a reason they had wanted a quick sale. We cleared up the permit question with the town for a few thousand dollars by having an architect and electrician sign off on the dormer. And as for that $17,000 estimate for termite remediation, one of my guys did the work for $1,200. After two months, the house was renovated and ready to sell.

We listed the house for sale, and one of my partners' agents soon was showing it to an excited young couple. They saw an attractive, newly renovated, dormered cape, with three bedrooms, two baths, and hardwood floors, in a good school district and with good train service. They could see it was a good buy for them.

Then the agent noticed that as the couple left in their car, the neighbor flagged them down and started chatting with them. Later, when the agent made a follow-up call to the couple, they told her that they really liked the house but that, well, the neighbor warned them about termite problems and told them to watch out because it had been a really quick renovation.

My partner Mark called me at home, and I exploded. I'm a lot calmer than I was in those days—I'm a Buddhist monk now by comparison. We'd done a great job on that house, and we'd treated that guy better than he deserved, and now this? I told my wife that I was going to pay that neighbor a visit. She suggested that might not be a good idea, but I insisted.

I banged on his door and asked him to step outside, away from his wife. He looked horrified that I was there.

"Listen, I went out of my way to be polite to you, and now I understand that you interfered with the sale of our property," I told him. "If you cause a problem again, I'll have my attorney sue you, and if you interfere with the sale of this house, I'll turn it into a Section 8 welfare rental, and I'll personally cut the grass maybe once a year when it's eight feet high!"

"I didn't say anything bad about your place," he protested. It's hard to get a liar to man up. There was no chance that the couple who declined to buy the house had made up a story with those details.

"Good," I told him. "That means we won't be having any further conversations about this."

I wasn't looking for a fight. I was looking to make sure he knew I wouldn't tolerate that. Some things you just need to deal with face to face. He tried to backpedal, not very convincingly, and I left him there looking dumbfounded. We never had another problem with him. The house quickly sold to another couple. We had done a beautiful renovation with professional contractors. We passed a termite inspection and repaired all damages.

This was a bitter, jealous guy, and you will run into such sorts. He was sitting at home and going nowhere, and he was jealous of our success. If you're investing in real estate and begin to succeed, some people may try to trip you up. It might be a neighbor, or it might be a relative. They hate that you are doing what they aren't doing, or can't do. Don't let clowns try to crush your opportunities. Confront them. You might not want to do it the way I did. I'd be more diplomatic today, perhaps. You could have your lawyer write a warning letter. But don't tolerate people like that, ever. I never do. They're a poison.

That's an extreme case. Jealousy is more likely to be subtle: "That's never going to work," people will say, or, "You can't do this." Yes, you can. Tommy may not be doing it because he's sitting on the couch all day drinking beers and watching football games, but you can do it. So, don't let nosy, pushy neighbors interfere with the sale of a property, and don't let relatives or neighbors or colleagues talk you out of something you're interested in doing. Don't let small people talk you out of big opportunities.

Don't let small people talk you out of big opportunities.

And don't let small problems frustrate you to the point of giving up. They might seem like beatings, but you can take it: They're really mostly distractions and interruptions. We were rehabbing a house recently and the first day on the job, a neighbor approached us and pointed to the car of one of our workers that was parked in front of her house—on the public street. "Make sure that's out of here when my husband gets home at 4," she demanded. It was 7:30 in the morning. So we moved the car. We're not looking to bang heads with people. It's not worth it.

Remember your vision. Dealing with a difficult person now and then should never make you lose sight of that vision. Not only will you be making good money, but you'll be improving neighborhoods and communities, getting houses back on the tax rolls, and fulfilling the dreams of first-time home buyers and people looking to move up. Investing in distressed real estate is not only lucrative, it is also immensely satisfying.

CHAPTER 5

Check Points

When I was a cop in the 103rd Precinct in Jamaica about twenty years ago, a group of us did steady 4-to-12 shifts. Sometimes when we got off work at midnight, we'd go out. I wasn't usually part of that group because I normally had to get up early the next day for my construction job, but sometimes we would go out for a few drinks after a shift. They used to call those shifts "4-to-4's" because you'd start work at 4 in the afternoon, get off at midnight, and go out until 4 when the bars closed.

It was at about 4 o'clock one morning when four or five of us, after leaving a bar called Ryan's in the precinct, decided it would be a good idea to go to Chinatown to Wo Hop (which is still a favorite restaurant of mine. I bring my kids into the city a couple of times a year for shopping on Canal Street and lunch at Wo Hop). This particular morning, after the 4-12 shift, I was there with the group as we continued to indulge.

When it was time to leave, one of the guys was missing. He was no longer at the table. We called him "Dr. Jekyll and Mr. Claven" because before he became a police officer he had been a mailman like Cliff Claven on "Cheers," and when he had a couple of drinks he became Dr. Jekyll, a lunatic. Normally he was a calm and well-behaved guy.

We staggered up the stairs to Mott Street about 5 a.m. In the late '80s, Chinatown had big gang problems. We heard a loud dispute and looked down an alley to where Dr. Jekyll had been urinating on a door. It was not a good idea. It happened to be the door of a gambling den controlled by a violent Chinatown gang called the Ghost Shadows Club. Four or five of the members were taking tremendous offense to his choice of places to relieve himself.

Most people would quickly retreat, but Dr. Jekyll wasn't thinking clearly enough for that, if he was thinking at all. He felt that maybe he was in a position to argue the case. I was able to mediate a retreat nonetheless, offered an apology, and we all backed out safely and returned to our homes. Some of us were armed, I'm sure, and I'm confident that most of the Ghost Shadows were, as well. So a retreat was the wise choice. May sober heads always prevail.

The lesson here is, "When you're outgunned, back off." It applies at many times and places in life besides 5 a.m. in Chinatown. In real estate, I made a tactical retreat from late 2007 until late 2009 because it was no longer safe to buy properties in my market and do what I like to do. I wasn't going to put my money or any of my investors' money at risk at that time. I was outgunned, so I went to the sidelines.

We're involved in multiple businesses, so it was time to focus more on the construction end and on the listing of bank-owned properties, but it was not safe to buy. It wasn't the right time to be in that field, so I made a tactical retreat from real estate for a couple of years—from the distressed end of it, anyway.

> **The lesson is: "When you're outgunned, back off." It applies at many times and places in life besides 5 a.m. in Chinatown. In real estate, I made a tactical retreat from late 2007 until late 2009.**

When you find yourself in the wrong place or at the wrong time, whether it's a Chinatown alley or the real estate market, take a look at where you're at, be honest about the situation, and when it's time to back off, back off. I'd had a good stretch of raising capital and generating income. I didn't want to flush that down the toilet by chasing a receding market. Don't try to catch a falling knife, as they say.

You can see the trends. The signals are clear, if you're paying attention, or if you're working with an agent or broker who is paying attention. In late 2007, it should have been clear to anyone that it was not safe to buy homes. Lenders had been giving loans at 120 or 125 percent loan-to-value to people with no documentable income. People who never should have been given a mortgage were getting them. The market was unstable, and prices were rising at a ridiculous rate as the bubble grew.

That's the point where the smart money says, "Enough. This is going to burst, and we don't want to be around when it does." I exited the market, so I didn't lose any money, and none of the investors who work with me lost any money. Some people want to stay in the real estate game no matter what is going on in the economy, but it's simply unwise not to heed the signals. When the market is moving 25 or 35 percent against you, it's impossible to be profitable. Common sense tells you to put your capital to the side once in a while. By late 2009 and early 2010, we still had our capital to get back in the game.

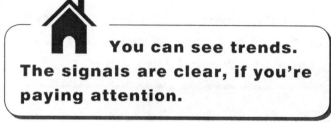

You can see trends. The signals are clear, if you're paying attention.

I knew people in the business who were jammed with multiple properties that they couldn't unload. They bought at the top of the market. They thought that the Greater Fool Theory would work for them—that some bigger fool than them would come along and buy them out—but that didn't happen.

It's like musical chairs when the music stops and there's nowhere to sit. The result, for many, has been a painful parade of bankruptcies and foreclosures. Had they paid attention to the signals, they would have been well positioned for the many great deals available today. Unfortunately, their capital now has vanished. Any investors they once had are no longer confident in them.

Usually when you think it's a good time for a tactical retreat, it is. That's true on Wall Street, Main Street, or in a back alley. When you start to feel uneasy, usually it's a good time to get out. Nobody has a crystal ball on the economy, but you can still get a clear idea of things to come. What is the market telling you? How long are houses taking to sell? Are the prices rising, or have they hit a peak and begun to trend down? Real estate doesn't plunge in value overnight the way stocks sometimes do. The change is slow. Even if losses are severe, the drain is likely to take two or three years, not two or three days. If you pay attention to the multiple listing service data, you will have time to adjust and secure your position.

If you nonetheless ignore the obvious signs and buy at the top of the market, don't cry when you see prices heading down. If you fail to make a tactical retreat, don't whine when your money and your investors are gone. If you were at The Dock in Montauk, you can be sure that George would hustle you out the door.

THE FORREST GUMP OF REAL ESTATE

When we were buying a lot of auction properties, a group of guys called one of the buyers the "Forrest Gump of real estate." If you've seen that movie, you'll recall that things somehow managed to work out for Forrest, one way or another. Larry was like that. He bought a lot of houses and was usually able to sell them.

Then there was Dino, a professional, savvy real estate broker and investor who frequented the foreclosure auctions. He and his team did outstanding due diligence on any property that they were buying. If Dino was bidding, most other people would feel confident bidding. The man is a pro who really does his homework.

Larry's system apparently was to do what Dino did, except for the due diligence. He didn't even look at the properties in advance. He figured he could save time by just showing up at the auctions, and if Dino was bidding he'd bid against him, presuming that Dino knew his stuff. Larry's system was far from advisable, but the market was rising, and as the saying goes, a rising tide lifts all boats.

Larry once was driving down Montauk Highway and happened to see Dino's car turning into the town of Islip. Larry figured there must be an auction, so he screamed a U-turn. He had no idea which property Dino wanted, but felt like being in the game.

There was in fact an auction, and I was there, too. Dino was interested in a property in Brentwood. The bank's minimum price, also called the upset price, was $117,000, as listed in the foreclosure profiles that came out about three weeks before the auction. However, the house had since burned to the ground. At the time of the auction, nothing remained but the foundation and a burnt shell.

Dino or someone from his team had gone to the property the day before, as usual. He knew about the fire and had come to the auction only because he was interested in the value of the land. A lot of times, the banks will adjust dramatically in such situations. He was prepared to pay $50,000 for the building lot.

Larry knew none of that because he was following his usual tack of doing as Dino did, and he knew that Dino had his eye on that property. When the bidding opened at the minimum $117,000, Larry immediately jumped in at $117,100, figuring $100 over the bank's upset price would undoubtedly be a good deal. He waited for Dino to top him.

But that's where it ended. Dino did not bid: He was only going to bid if the bank had dropped the upset price. Larry was the winner. He bid $117,100 for a foundation and some charred debris, as he no doubt discovered later when he drove out to see his prize. To buy at an auction in our area, you have to leave 10 percent in cash or certified check with the referee. That money is nonrefundable: If you don't follow through with a purchase, you don't get that money back. The bank keeps it. Larry forfeited nearly $12,000.

> **Many people just follow the crowd. If everyone's buying, they jump in. That's a losing strategy.**

"Stupid is as stupid does," Forrest Gump would say. That was the day things didn't work out for Larry. His lack of due diligence cost him dearly. Later, when the market tanked, he was caught with a slew of overpriced properties that he had bought at the top of the market. He's no longer in the business. The economy flushed him out, along with others who didn't know what they were doing. Dino, by contrast, is a disciplined bidder who stops when he hits his price point. He does his homework and his math and is faithful to the numbers. He knows what he is buying.

There are too few Dinos out there. Many people just follow the crowd. If everyone's buying, they jump in. That's a losing strategy. At the top of the market in 2007, the crowd was buying like mad, imagining 50 percent returns the next year. What many actually got was quite the opposite. They just reached into that box of chocolates without knowing what they were going to get. You may want a caramel, but if you get a marshmallow, remember: no crying babies.

SOUND CHECK AT THE GREEN PARROT

Once a year, I get together in Key West, Florida, for a fishing trip with my old NYPD partner, Greg Allgeier, who lives in Michigan now. Everyone calls him Augie. Whether or not we get a good catch, we do catch up on each other's lives. He's long been a close friend.

We always stop at a bar called the Green Parrot, a popular place among the locals where terrific bands play on Friday and Saturday nights. At 5 o'clock on Fridays, the band does a sound check at a time when Key West people are stopping in after work. For an hour or so, the band performs as it works out any kinks with its crew. The locals like to show up for the sound check. It's a real show in a cool venue, without the crowds that show up later.

These musicians are professionals. They are popular bands that travel the country and take their art seriously. Five hours before their gig, they run through the songs they will be doing that evening. That's how much they care about their reputation.

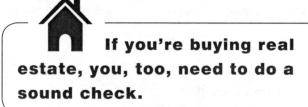

If you're buying real estate, you, too, need to do a sound check.

If you're buying real estate, you, too, need to do a sound check. Are your decisions in line with your long-term goals? You need to constantly review your buying system and update it. As I explained, it's critical that you have a system so that you know how to review any property that you are thinking about buying. You need to know where to get accurate data, calculate your costs, and lock in your profit. But that's not enough: You need to monitor the situation and do any necessary fine tuning and updating.

Based on what's happening in the market, I may change my song. Like the musicians at the Green Parrot, I want to make sure I'm ready for the real show. That holds true no matter what your angle is in the real estate business. If you're buying property to hold and plan to rent it out, you need to regularly update your system. How high will your rents be? What's the vacancy rate for similar apartments in your area? Is the employment rate in your region rising or falling? Are businesses opening or closing? You'll want to know these things before you invest in an apartment complex.

Because what I do is buy, renovate, and resell, my sound check involves looking at what the housing market is telling me about prices. Can I be reasonably assured of my 17 to 20 percent profit, after expenses? That's my system, and though it has worked for me for two decades now, I'm constantly modifying it.

For example, I regularly update my pricing guide—the one that you can find at RehabandGrowRich.com—as the market changes, since it is a crucial element in making sure that my profit projections are correct. Nobody can make good decisions without knowing how much things cost. How much more might you pay for an air conditioning system today compared with two years ago? Has there been a plywood shortage that has pushed up prices? What's the going rate for labor, and are your contractors aligned with that? There are so many factors that influence costs—among them inflation, industry trends, supply and demand—and you must keep abreast of them. You need the right figures for your formula.

When I did my sound check in late in 2007, I turned down the volume. In fact, I pulled the plug. The market was telling me that it was no longer safe to do my type of business. I turned the volume back up a few years later, when I began buying aggressively again.

But I check all the meters. I review my set list, and I play to the audience. I watch my numbers.

YOUR PERSONAL SOUND CHECK

An important consideration, when checking your buying system, is to make sure that you are attending to both your long-term and short-term goals. I invest both in cash accounts and with my self-directed IRA. Each has its place as I plan for my family's future.

I'm in my mid-40s and certainly want the IRA to grow. I don't intend to touch the money for at least twenty years, and I want to have many millions in it when I'm ready to retire and help my family and children. That's long-term money.

But there are times when I'm going to focus more on my cash accounts and my short-term expenses. I have a daughter in college, and I have two more who will be in college in the next couple of years, so now I'm going to put a little bit more cash account money into real estate deals. I will take some profits, pay taxes on them, and use that to fund my daughters' educations and our daily living expenses.

> **Having a good strategy involves a lot more than whether it is a safe time to buy or not. What funds will you be using to make a purchase? Are you using your own capital or bringing in additional investor capital?**

Seven or eight years from now, when my daughters are all out of college, I'll be focusing more on my real estate within my self-directed IRA. Once those years of heavy tuition bills are over, I'm going to be looking to supercharge my IRA so that I'm funding a great retirement for myself and my wife.

Having a good strategy involves a lot more than whether it is a safe time to buy or not. What funds will you be using to make a purchase? Are you using your own capital or bringing in additional investor capital? I'm doing that, as well, now because there are a lot of good opportunities. From 2007 to 2009, I backed off from some of my private investors. Now that opportunities have reappeared, we're not only using the previous investors who have worked with us, but we're actually bringing in some new friends and family and others who want to make 8 to 10 percent returns either in their cash accounts or IRAs.

With the IRAs, your investments are tax-deferred and continually compound until you start taking distributions. You can take withdrawals without penalty after age 59½, but they are not required until you are 70½. If you would like to learn more about getting started with self-directed IRA investments for maximum return, specifically in real estate, I recommend *IRA Wealth: Revolutionary IRA Strategies for Real Estate Investment* by Patrick W. Rice. It will help you make your personal sound check.

I'm going to be using my self-directed IRA my whole life. There may come a time where I don't want to be involved personally with buying and renovating distressed properties. I may at that point say, "I'm going to write mortgages," and, with several million dollars, lend money to others for their real estate deals. There are many opportunities, and Rice's book explores how you can take advantage of them to grow your retirement account.

Another book that I have found highly informative is Ralph Roberts' *Real Wealth by Investing in Real Estate*. He's a Michigan-based real estate broker and investor with a broad range of advice, whether you want to buy properties to flip or for rentals.

When I first started as a police officer, we had a 401(k) plan with very minimal options, but I started putting $600 a month into one of the few choices that we had. When I retired from the police after 20 years, I had a few hundred thousand dollars in there that I was able to roll into a self-directed IRA and use for real estate deals. Everyone should start some type of investment early in his or her working career. Nobody can know everything. The world of finances and financial planning is daunting to people, and they make some huge mistakes. It might be an area where you want to get some financial counseling, especially early in your life, long before you retire.

You should also look for your niche early in life and learn as much as you can, whether it's about distressed real estate or something else. Find a vehicle that can provide you with a good life throughout your working years and provide you with a comfortable and secure retirement. My daughters have attended summer programs at Harvard and Brown where they have met people from around the world and been introduced to new ideas. Young people need to see the opportunities that are out there so they can decide what they want to pursue.

I recently joined a group called *Strategic Coach*. It's an executive development program and works mainly with entrepreneurs. We meet quarterly in Chicago to exchange best practices and tools and concepts for business and personal growth. My coach is Lee Brower, who wrote *The Brower Quadrant*. One of the things he talks about is eliminating areas of frustration. We all hit what is known as a Ceiling of Complexity—we reach a certain income level and can't rise above that because of the frustrations we face. The solution is to embrace the positives.

At those Chicago meetings, I interact with people from around the country involved in a broad and diverse group of businesses. I'm primarily in the real estate and construction business, along with education. Others are financial planners, some of them are doctors, and some of them are in insurance. The lessons are universal and valuable to us all.

CHAPTER 6

Make Sure You Salute

Back in the 103rd Precinct, we had a newly promoted police chief who lived in the community. The day after he was promoted from inspector, he came in to visit the precinct and walked in wearing civilian clothes. Nobody had any idea who he was.

He walked up to the desk where a sergeant and an officer handling the phones were sitting. The officer glanced up but barely noticed him. The chief turned to the sergeant, who finally said: "Can I help you?"

"When I walk into this command," the chief said, "I want everybody snapping to attention and saluting me." He was outraged. He felt he should have been recognized, though he wasn't even in uniform. Because there were almost 40,000 people in the police department at the time, it would have been unlikely that anyone would know his face. So nobody was saluting. Nobody was jumping to attention. The chief didn't like that.

The police department has an inspections unit, which comes down to precincts to hammer them: "Your hair's too long" or "You didn't shave this morning" or "You're wearing white socks instead of black socks." These guys descended on the precinct the day after the chief was snubbed and brought up a bunch of minor infractions and violations. The chief had spoken.

> **In my practice, I salute—that is, I stay in people's good graces and show respect. It's the right thing to do, and it's good for business.**

Soon, pictures of the chief appeared all over the precinct with the notice, "This is our chief. If you see him, please salute." Someone also thought it would be a pretty good idea to put his picture on some urinal deodorizer pucks. It wasn't long before the chief was looking up at every officer in the precinct.

I don't necessarily recommend that as the best way to deal with these situations. You need to look out for the people on your team, and everyone you deal with, and be respectful of them. In my practice, I salute—that is, I stay in people's good graces and show respect. It's the right thing to do, and it's good for business.

You should be polite and courteous and respectful, whether you're buying a home from a distressed seller, or whether you're working with a contractor. Life is much easier that way. You should salute certain people even when you'd prefer not to. I'm going to stay in the good graces of building inspectors, plan examiners, and anybody else I'm involved with who feels important.

You'll run into buffoons in the business. A lot of building inspectors, for some reason, are vertically challenged, but when they come to the job they think they're Andre the Giant. They want to be bowed to like a king, and they have the ability to stop your job or make it much more difficult. A plans examiner, too, has that power.

As a practice, I try to be a nice guy, and when I'm dealing with one of these people I'm even nicer. Sometimes it's annoying to have to be nice to rude people, but I never forget the power wielded by people in the building departments. Almost all of what I do involves working on distressed real estate and sometimes enlarging houses. If I'm converting a Cape into a Colonial, I must deal with a plans examiner who's going to look at the architectural drawings. Then at every step of the process, I will deal with a building inspector who comes out and looks at the framing and the electric and plumbing and insulation and the whole package.

It's not a big deal. We have great relationships with them, but they're a group that needs to be saluted. You don't have to put their picture on a urinal puck deodorizer, but when you get to know them, make sure you're polite, make sure you're out-of-your-way courteous. Be humble.

Building inspectors usually are not paid that well. They may be making $45,000 or $50,000. They're very eager to find out what kind of numbers are possible in the business of distressed real estate, which I always downplay. I say, "You can barely make a living. After all the expenses, there's almost nothing there." This would not be the group to which you might say: "Hey! I just made $45,000 flipping this house, and we're working on three others!"

In fact, be very careful about saying that to anyone. Yes, there is much money to be made. But that's not a conversation you want to have with people in the building departments, or with your subcontractors. I tell those people that I'm grinding it out, just like everybody else. I would be more candid with the investor about the numbers, at least so that they know how their investment is secured with you. But I wouldn't talk finances with a subcontractor, and I certainly wouldn't dress in a way that might make him think about inflating the bill.

When you're going into town halls looking for tax records, be polite to all whose paths you cross. These mostly are people on fixed salaries. They don't want to be entrepreneurial. They don't want to take the risks and the steps that are involved with what we do, but they also don't want to hear that you made $250,000 last year when they made $45,000 while grinding it out every day.

It's important to keep your projects moving, and that's one of the main reasons that it is important to salute people who feel important. If somebody annoys you, you may be tempted to draw a line in the sand, as friends of mine have done, saying, "Screw them. I'm not kissing this guy's ass." Not a good idea. Nothing works for you if your job gets stopped.

I remember a line from a book that we were given to read in the police department. It was called *Verbal Judo*, and it was about how to defuse situations: "If it feels good, no good." If you're in a confrontation and tell an inspector what you believe he should go do to himself, it feels good. But it's no good. He has the power to stop your project. Every future inspection you get is going to be difficult. He's going to be talking to the six or seven other inspectors in his office, saying, "This guy's a dick." When dealing with civil servants and government employees, follow the rule that if what you want to say would feel good, it's usually a good idea not to say it. Be humble, and you'll get much better results.

DO THINGS RIGHT THE FIRST TIME, PERMISSION VS. FORGIVENESS

Sometimes you'll hear people say that when it comes to permits, it's better to ask for forgiveness than for permission because people can tell you no. For many years, I would do some projects without building permits. These days we're doing bigger projects, such as adding second stories. Clearly you need a permit because when you go to sell, you need to have a certificate of occupancy.

In my area, you may have to get a survey and get architectural drawings submitted. If you start work without securing these things, they can charge you twice the fee. I had one stop work order where I was supposed to have a $700 permit. Because I had already started, they doubled it. It became $1,400. I generally am working with a building permit these days.

If you're watching the HGTV shows, you'll never see a building permit. You'll never see a building inspector. Multiple things are happening at the same time, yet you don't see permits. I'm not saying that can't be the case: I've done many projects in place over the years—not additions where you are adding rooms or second stories—and in such cases a permit sometimes is not required.

If the renovations that you are doing involve painting, new carpets, cleaning, and perhaps roofing, windows and siding, you may not need a permit. More often, permits are required when plumbing and electrical work is involved. If you're gutting a bathroom to the studs in my area, and installing new plumbing and electrical wiring, you won't need a building permit, but you will need a plumbing and electrical permit. I certainly need building permits when adding second stories or repairing fire damage and other major jobs.

> The inspectors are doing their job, and they lose work if you don't get a permit. They can clobber you. So do things right.

Some buyers do what they call lipstick renovation where they're just doing a cleanup. I don't feel that those projects make as much money when you sell, but they work for some. For these projects, you clearly do not need a building permit. If you are doing a gut renovation, you do. For many other projects, you may not be so certain, so you will need to check into the situation. It's not a perfect science.

I bought a house in Eastport, New York, with an attached garage that was rotted. The garage had been converted into what should have been a good master suite. It was a two-bedroom, one-bath primary house with an attached former barn, which could become a really cool space with a walk-in closet and big bathroom. That's what my intention was. I'd been on a roll. It was all on the certificate of occupancy that these buildings were there, so I thought, "I could knock this out."

We went in there and blasted away, gutted the property, and had a container on the job for the debris. I later learned that the seller's brother was a local contractor who saw us working and reported us to the Southampton Building Department. I guess it was a case of sour grapes that his brother didn't sell the house to him, or perhaps he just didn't like to see some other contractor working there. You'll run into that. It isn't necessarily that the authorities have a GPS on your properties. It can be a case of nosy neighbors or jealous contractors or others who for some reason find satisfaction in reporting you, even when it's unjustified. Your job can be interrupted just the same.

In this case, my brother, Phil, was on the job site managing a few men when a building inspector showed up. I was driving somewhere when Phil called to tell me an inspector wanted to know if there was a permit. I thought I'd be cute: "Tell him yeah we just got the permit and we'll call when we want an inspection." The inspector wasn't amused. There was no permit, he said, and if he wanted he could give me a $10,000 fine for operating without a permit. I certainly didn't have one—I hadn't been to the building department.

I had to get a survey and architect's drawings, and submit them to the Town of Southampton. Our project was shut down for two months. I was stuck with two months of carrying costs on the property, and it cost me $1,600 just in taxes to let the property sit for those two months. The experience underscored a lesson I should have known all too well. You must salute these people. I didn't play it smart.

Doing things properly doesn't slow you down if you coordinate properly. Let's say I'm buying your house today, with closing six weeks away. If I can get my architect to come in right away, his drawing and the permit can both be ready by the time of closing. It's not complicated, and that's what I do now.

In some parts of the country, I'm told, you can do as you wish. No inspectors show up. I don't have experience elsewhere. My experience on

Long Island is that you can be shut down. It happens routinely. Once you start work, you can expect a visit from the building department. The inspectors are doing their job, and they lose work if you don't get a permit. They can be vindictive, and they can clobber you. So do things right. You should be using licensed contractors anyway whose work will easily pass any inspection—and keep your project flowing smoothly.

SURROUND YOURSELF WITH THE RIGHT PEOPLE

My old police partner Augie—that fishing buddy I meet once a year in the Keys— told me he was going to write a book called *Extended Tour, Portal to Portal* about his experiences and adventures in the department. He had plenty. He had quite an "extended tour," which is how the police refer to a prolonged assignment beyond the usual. "Portal to portal" means overtime in both directions for travel time to a detail—an 8½-hour day could become an 11-hour day, for example.

In the real estate business, "Extended Tour, Portal to Portal" makes me think of the spectrum of people you deal and work with—the property owners and the investors, the lawyers and the contractors, the bankers and all the folks around the settlement table. Many individuals need to work in concert to make a deal happen. You need a dependable team.

Your inner circle will include your accountant, of course, and in most states an attorney, and it's best to have one with particular expertise in the real estate business. You want an attorney whose business is focused exclusively or largely on real estate and who understands investor/client relationships. You must speak the same language. My attorney, Lance Longo, who has served me well for fifteen years, closes more than 200 real estate transactions a year, whereas I go to ten in a good year. He's able to get the most difficult properties to close. I have yet to see him stumped by a question. With that experience and education, he's invaluable to me. He has encountered everything that will come up in a closing, and it's a pleasure to have someone like that on the team.

Your partners will be an integral part of your investing business—I think of the role that Mark and Rich played in my early career, and the importance of the partners that I have had since. I've had partners with whom I split the profits after the deal, and today I have wealth partners who invest in my deals for an 8 or 10 percent return on their investment but don't partake in the profits.

Your insurance broker is critical. I'm amazed when I hear that people—even some friends of mine—haven't gotten insurance on their properties. It's terribly shortsighted. Occasionally, and maybe very rarely, something will happen, but do you want to take that chance?

I wouldn't consider buying a property without a policy on it. A lot of the properties that I buy will not qualify for traditional insurance that you might get if you bought a house in good condition, like a regular Allstate or State Farm policy. In those cases, my broker gets me what's called a Builder's Risk Policy. It does a good job of insuring your property while the renovation is under way. I always have insurance on my properties, and I don't think it's an option to skip it.

Together, you're better. Your team members will facilitate your ability to do more and better deals.

If you're not an agent or a broker yourself, you should have those people on your team to help you locate properties and find the deals. You will need an inner circle of contractors whom you trust to stay in line with your pricing guide. Early on, you may work with a general contractor who coordinates things for you, but very quickly you want to become your own general contractor. I serve that role, and I'm a contractor as well.

You will have a roofing contractor and a kitchen crew. You will have a plumber and electrician and various other tradesmen. Think of them all as your partners. Sometimes in a construction renovation project, we may have seven or eight trades coming in. They're a critical part of the team. So are the people who handle the property sale.

The inner circle is the main team of people with whom you will be working for the long haul on just about every project. That's why you must screen them carefully so that you have experience and integrity on your side. And when you find such people, you will want to salute them again and again.

MAKE SURE YOUR HEAD DOESN'T EXPLODE

One frustration that I have felt is that I'm not delegating enough. I find myself doing administrative and secretarial tasks that could be delegated to people at $15 to $25 an hour, while I'm looking to make $250 an hour. I'm doing low-value tasks. Surround yourself with a team that can do that work for you as well as take care of responsibilities that aren't in your area of expertise or interest. Together, you're better. Your team members may not be your direct employees, but they will facilitate your ability to do more and better deals.

Another way that I was able to pursue more project was to deal with another frustration: For a long time, I believed that if I only had $100,000, I could only do $100,000 in deals. Then I opened up the opportunity for investors to do business with me, and I found that I could have partners in wealth who would make an 8 or 10 percent return on my deals. That expanded the possibilities.

Before I joined the Strategic Coach group, I used to measure myself against my ideal. If your ideal is to have $5 million in investor capital and you have only raised $3 million, you're constantly frustrated. What this group teaches you is to set your goals forward, but measure your progress backwards. I look backwards and say, "Well, four years ago I had no money in private investor capital, and today I have $3 million." I'm moving in the direction of my ideal, and I'm happy about my progress because this is what I've done. Move forward and measure backwards.

The group urges us to start everything with a positive focus. Focus on what's positive in your life, what you're happy with, what's working for you. Avoid negative self-talk. A lot of that stems from not being at your ideal location and ultimate goal. But that really never happens for anybody. You can walk forever toward the horizon, but can you catch it? At dinner, my wife and the girls and I strive to say something positive that happened that day or to talk about something we're excited about. It encourages a better chain of thought. Thinking about what's wrong and what you don't have will stifle your creativity and stifle your growth.

The Strategic Coach program has helped me in many ways. Lee Brower is a terrific coach. He was featured in *The Secret*, a book and DVD that was popular a few years ago. It was from him that I learned the importance of delegating. The program teaches that you should spend most of your time on your unique ability—and when you're not spending time on your unique ability, your frustration grows. My unique ability is not clerical and secretarial or computer work. It may be finding capital allocation opportunities in real estate.

> **Focus on what's positive in your life. Negativity often stems from not being at your ideal location and ultimate goal. But that really never happens for anybody. You can walk forever toward the horizon, but can you catch it?**

Some people feel that if they're in charge, they have to do it all. You can't do it all—at least not well. Each of us has just a few areas of expertise. To the extent that we're very strong in one area, we're probably going to be very weak in another area. You need to delegate your weak areas to those who enjoy that work and are highly competent. Some people are good at carpentry, others at negotiating. You need them all on your team.

Maurice Flannery from Coverage Concepts is an insurance broker whom I've used for about fifteen years. He insures, coordinates, or brokers the coverage of all of my real estate deals. I don't know anything about doing that. I'm not an insurance broker, and I don't want to be one, but I do want to make sure that my investments and my investors' investments are secured.

I am a real estate broker. I list and sell my own properties almost always. Occasionally I'll list with another broker who has brought me a good deal, or if it's a deal within my self-directed IRA (for a list of transactions prohibited within your IRA, such as self-dealing, visit RehabandGrowRich.com). In addition, I have a network of subcontractors in every trade. I consider all those guys to be partners. They're not joint venturing with me on the deal, but they are partners in profit with me. They're profiting from doing the roofing and siding, and I'm profiting on the ultimate sale of the house.

I might meet a potential investor for lunch or a round of golf and talk a little bit about it, but you won't find me taking phone calls from people inquiring about buying a property: That's handled by my real estate office, and an agent is doing that. I'm getting away, more and more, from the paperwork and any of what I consider the frustrating and annoying pieces of my business that can be delegated to somebody who gets paid for the job.

You need to figure out where you're comfortable and where the money comes from in your business. In my business, it comes from my ability to locate good deals, coordinate the construction and wholesale prices, work with investors who want to do business with me, and make sure that I have the right people to work with me. That's where I'm spending my time.

WHERE THE SMART MONEY IS

It comes down to this: You can always bring in somebody else to put up with the crap. You shouldn't be doing your own renovations even if you are a master carpenter. I know that I bring in the bucks by looking for new deals and raising private investor capital.

That is really where the money is. The money isn't saved by being Mr. and Mrs. Hands-On and doing everything yourself. I don't get involved, physically, in any of the work on the jobs that I do. I coordinate them and manage them, I make phone calls, and do some supervision. I check in after the job is done and make sure I am happy with it and then write a check, but there is no reason to physically be doing the work. You don't have to be the guy with the hammer and the screw gun. There is no money in that. Those guys make $20 an hour. You want to make $200 an hour.

> **If you are spending an entire work day at one house, ripping up flooring yourself, you probably won't make it to the foreclosure auction where the deal of a lifetime could be waiting.**

I have a friend who wants to be hands on. On one job, he could not get the tile guy on the job quickly, so he did it himself. He tiled two bathrooms, and it was absolutely awful. He is not a tile guy. Most people are not. They over-judge their own skills and minimize the difficulty. My friend ruined the price of his house. Everybody who walked in and saw the bathrooms said to themselves, "Wow, what a butcher job."

You can't fool the market when you do it yourself. Even if you are a master carpenter, you waste time by spending two months on the job when instead you could be finding deals. If you aren't qualified, you may think you saved money and imagine you did a good job, but when the potential buyers proclaim the workmanship to be shoddy, the sales price will fall accordingly. I see it over and over again.

The lesson is simple: Don't do work on your own jobs. Instead, learn more about real estate. Look at more properties. Market your own properties. Work with investors.

VALUE YOUR TIME

I wasted a lot of time early in my career. Several things held me back. One was not thinking big enough about how much I could accomplish. The other was not raising private capital early enough. When my partners and I ran out of our own money on hand, that was the end of the game until we sold a house. And I spent way too much time doing the physical work myself. I was doing $20-an-hour work when I wanted to be making many multiples of that.

You have to say, "I have this much time in the day. I want to make this much an hour." Divide how much you want to earn in a year by the number of work hours in a year, and that's the hourly rate you should strive to receive. Everything that you do has to be worth that much or more. If it is worth less, you need to delegate the work. If cleanup work can be done for $12 an hour and you want to make $100 an hour, then somebody else has to get the $12 an hour job while you concentrate on more profitable and bigger things.

Economists refer to the "opportunity cost" of not using your assets—whether financial or intellectual—to their maximum. Don't waste time or money on pursuits that earn less than you are capable of making. Think of the time value of money, and don't squander it.

> **Think big. Don't think about how you can save $15. Think about how you can make $15,000.**

I am looking to turn properties as quickly as I can. I want the money back, and I want it to be constantly moving when the opportunities are good, which they are now. There are times to retreat, as I have explained, but not lately: You want to be back in the game, and when you're on your knees spreading grout, you're putting yourself on the sidelines. Think big. Don't think about how you can save $15. Think about how you can make $15,000.

CHAPTER 7

Kicked in the Nuts, and Other Lessons to Remember

"Security, holding one," the dispatcher said, calling me to a shoplifting arrest. The words told me that a store security guard had apprehended someone and probably had the suspect in handcuffs. The store was around the block from my foot post. I headed over.

When I walked in, I saw that store security had detained a woman. She was petite, probably under 100 pounds, maybe five feet tall. Her hands were cuffed behind her, and a burly security guard stood next to her, his hand on her shoulder. "We caught her shoplifting. We arrested her," he announced to me.

I walked right up to her, nonchalantly. In a flash, the woman's foot was in motion: She kicked me square in the nuts, and I fell to my knees. She hadn't seemed threatening at all, but because she caught me off guard, she was able to drop me, and I'm six feet tall, 225 pounds.

It was out of the blue and totally preventable. Now when I'm meeting people for the first time, I remember how much it hurt to be kicked in the nuts, and so I stand sideways at first. And that goes for people I meet in real estate for the first time.

Once, in the early days of my real estate career, my partner Rich and I were talking to a shady character who had been buying and selling some houses. Rich was interested in a piece of property. "I own that property," the man told him, "and I will sell it to you for $110,000. You build a house and it'll be worth $450,000. So let's just scratch out a quick agreement." That should have been raising flags immediately, because in our area contracts go from attorney to attorney.

"Just give me $200 now," the man said, "and I'll have the attorney send over the contracts."

The deal never materialized. He didn't own the lot. For all we knew, he needed a quick $200 for drugs. That was a kick in the nuts. It's a consistent theme in the business of distressed real estate investing. Contractors might try to kick you. People looking to sell their properties might try to kick you.

That's another reason to have a really good attorney. I asked Lance about a seller who had been trying to deal with me. "Lance, do you know this guy?" I got a quick answer: "He's terrible. All his deals are shady. There are always title problems. Nothing is ever clear, it's always convoluted. I wouldn't touch him with a ten-foot pole." That was enough for me. What he offered sounded like a good deal, but if there were title issues and problems and he's known to be a bad guy to do business with, we're going to stay away from him and avoid getting kicked.

> ### Think big. Don't think about how you can save $15. Think about how you can make $15,000.

As a police officer, I never was kicked in the nuts again. That happened in my first year of service, and I spent twenty years in the department. I did stand sideways when approaching people just to prevent that from happening. One can't be too careful. In real estate, too, you need to watch out. There will be all kinds of bad deals. Sometimes things will seem too good to be true, and they are. It can be a dangerous business if you're not an informed student and you're not paying attention and learning from your experiences.

That goes back to my system. I avoid those swift kicks by doing the same thing over and over in real estate. I am successful. Systems lead to success in real estate and in life. Stay with your strengths. If I tried to go out and buy a CVS-anchored shopping mall or a strip mall with no idea how to manage it and what the numbers should be, I would be inviting problems. If I accepted contracts from bums, and not through attorneys, I would be inviting problems. I could get kicked.

There are a lot of people in every business, and some are disreputable. I've seen contractors with personal and behavior problems that prevent them from showing up day to day and doing what they need to do and finishing what they start. On first approach, be wary— and stand sideways.

"IF HIS TONGUE MOVES AGAIN, CUT IT"

There's another twist on that philosophy of "if it feels good, don't say it"—or, to borrow a line from the movie *The Deep* about undersea adventurers and the toothy perils they face: "If his tongue moves again, cut it." You can get yourself in trouble not only by disrespecting people in power, but also by flaunting your own success. I learned it from Donald Trump.

My friend Augie is a great organizer and would coordinate a lot of events during our days in the police precinct. He'd get a group of us to go out to a steakhouse each year for what we called the Christmas King Cut. This particular year, the King Cut was at the world-famous Peter Luger Steakhouse in Brooklyn. It probably wasn't the right venue for a bunch of struggling cops, but we would all go out and splurge a couple of times a year.

On that day, fifteen or twenty of us were in a side room, eating steaks and drinking, when we saw Trump exiting with an entourage of four or five people. Augie is irrepressible. He got up and he said: "Mr. Trump, the NYPD would just like to wish you a Merry Christmas." Trump was always a supporter of the cops. He donates to Cop Shot—if an officer is shot, he puts up $10,000 rewards for information leading to the arrest.

Trump came over to our table and shook hands with all of us, wishing us a Merry Christmas, and he was on his way. His entourage was a group of power players in real estate, and my group was a bunch of power drinkers in the police department. It felt good to be acknowledged personally—but this was not, however, the first time I met Trump.

A decade or so earlier when I was about 13 years old, I was caddying at Deepdale Country Club, an exclusive golf course on Long Island. It had only about 100 members, but they were high-powered players, including top investment bankers. There was an amazing amount of wealth at this place.

One day at a member guest tournament in 1980, Trump was golfing with a Texas oil guy named Jimmy Lynn. They arrived by helicopter that landed on the driving range, and I wound up caddying for the two of them for the round. They were both good golfers and great guys, and at the end of the round I got $100 from each of them. At the time, $50 was good, and $70 was great. Caddies felt they were doing well at $25 a bag. I got $200 from these two guys.

The caddy master was named Eddie Spegowski. We called him Eddie Specs. He was a retired postal worker, probably 75 at the time, and he had an adult son. I was 13. His son was in his 40s and was a banker or something, but on weekends he would come to this golf course and caddy. They let you play golf for free on Mondays, and guys were making $50 to $100 in cash for the day without working too hard.

> **Don't divulge information about your property deals. It's a highly competitive business, and you can easily give away your good fortunes.**

I heard that Trump and Lynn were looking to become members of the country club, so I piped up: "These guys are unbelievable!" I said. "Fantastic! I got $200 from them. Incredible!"

"Does Macy's tell Gimbel's what they do?" Eddie Specs asked me.

"What?"

"That means why are you telling everyone you got $200 when they got $50? There are times to keep your mouth shut."

The next year, Trump and Lynn returned for the tournament— and Eddie Specs gave the caddy job to his son. He got the choice "loop," as caddies call it. I caddied for a couple of guys who gave me $50. I liked Eddie, but he had taught me a lesson and had now charged me the tuition. He made sure I paid.

People want to boast about what they're doing and say, "Wow, I got this lead on a house where I think I can make $75,000. It's 14 Smith Street." It comes back to haunt them. You of course can talk about plans generally, but don't share your enthusiasm about specific properties and projects because there are a lot of people in this business and they may cut you out. If you see a really good deal, don't talk about it. I don't talk about my deals until they're closed. To me, it's not a deal until we've taken possession of the property.

Many people blow themselves up by talking too much about what they're going to do. Whether it's a good idea for an invention or a really good property that you're considering, don't talk about it. Keep it quiet until you have the deal locked up. I can still hear Eddie Specs' words: "There are times to keep your mouth shut." Don't divulge information about your property deals. It's a highly competitive business, and you can easily give away your good fortunes.

Nor should you brag about your investors. If I've identified Charlie Brown as an excellent investor for my real estate deals, I don't go running at the mouth that Charlie would be a terrific investor. There's probably half a dozen other guys who'd like to have him as an investor as well. I don't want anybody else soliciting him.

Remember: "If it feels good, no good." Keep your mouth shut. Listen to Eddie Specs.

I'LL GLADLY PAY YOU TUESDAY FOR A HAMBURGER TODAY

If you are familiar with the old Popeye cartoons, you know that the sailor man's portly friend Wimpy was fond of hamburgers and habitually short of cash. "I'll gladly pay you Tuesday for a hamburger today" was his signature line.

It's common in the construction business that people will ask for money advances. Some who have worked with me for many years must think I am Santa Claus. I'll get a call out of the blue from a contractor who works for me now and then, asking whether I might advance him $1,000 on the next job that he might do for me. My answer is no, and you should refuse, too, in most cases.

There are times when I will make exceptions. One of my sub-contractors called me one day, almost in a panic. His wife had an immigration issue, he said, and he needed $2,000 or she was going to be deported or detained. He did not have any friends or family in the United States that were in a position to help him. It wasn't clear why he needed the money—perhaps it was for an attorney's fee.

He'd worked for me for a number of years, so I wanted to lend him the money. I felt confident that he would square up his account because of the kind of guy he was, but even if he did not, I knew we'd had many hundreds of thousands of dollars in transactions between us. His concern seemed genuine.

He was delighted. I guess he had probably called all the other contractors that he worked with and they had turned him down. I gave it to him because I thought it was the right thing to do. I respected him and his work ethic and the relationship we had. I told him that we could square up when he was able. He has often done $7,000 to $8,000 jobs for me. We could have just adjusted it off one of those jobs.

You have to use your common sense. In this case, I liked the guy. I was sympathetic to his situation. He is from El Salvador, away from friends and family but hustling and getting a good business going here. I believed him when he said his wife was facing some immigration issues.

I thought of how my grandfather came from Ireland as a carpenter and eventually was a house builder, without his friends, family, or connections to help him. I was confident about my judgment of this man's character— and, as it turned out, I did get that money back, and he has continued to work with me these past several years. When you can do something like that, when you can help somebody in need, it really bonds a relationship.

I once did lend money to a tree trimmer who had done some work for me. A friend and fellow contractor who was putting a pool in my backyard had recommended him and vouched that he did terrific work—but warned me not to pay him a penny until the job was finished. If I paid him up front, he said, he might not return for months, if ever. But if I waited to pay him, my friend assured me, he would be prompt and diligent and knock the job out.

The trimmer quoted me a price of $5,000 but wanted $2,500 to start. "Sorry," I told him. "I'll be happy to pay you in full the day that you finish, but not a cent before that." He did indeed do a fine job, and he did a lot of other work for me.

Some years later, I got a call one day. He had not worked for me for a while.

"My truck's broken down in Kansas City," he told me, "and I need to get back to Long Island. Can you wire me $2,000?"

"I can't do that," I said.

"Well, what can you send me?" he persisted. I eventually consented to wire him $1,000. I didn't even know how to do that. He did. "Just go to a Wal-Mart there and they'll transfer the money to a Wal-Mart here in Kansas City." I did as he asked, but I figured I would never see that $1,000 again, unlike the money I had lent to the other contractor with the immigration issue. Still, he had done a tremendous amount of work for me over the years.

The following day, I was playing golf with my brother and a couple of other guys. My phone rang.

"Paul? Hey, it's me again. I'm broken down in Pennsylvania. Say, could you wire me another $1,000?"

It wasn't going to happen. I really didn't know where he was—he could have been in Long Island the whole time, for all I knew. I didn't see him for about a year after that, and I basically wrote off that $1,000 as never to be collected, which is what I expected when I sent him the money.

Last summer, though, I needed some cleanup work after a storm, so I looked him up and suggested that he might want to offer me $1,000 worth of work. And he did. He squared the account.

Those were a couple of times that I departed from my policy of not advancing money to people. You don't need to be the tough guy all the time, but use common sense. I would never do that for a contractor unless we had a longstanding relationship.

If I have never worked with someone before, no way will I pay anything in advance. If you download my A-Z Pricing Guide, you will also see our advice on dealing with contractors and how we go about it. If a roofing job takes one afternoon, I will inspect the job and then issue a check. You'll often hear from a contractor something like this: "I tell you what, just give me $3,000 now and you don't need to worry about the remaining $3,000 until we are done." Sorry, we don't do business in that fashion. "But we do have plenty of jobs that we could give you," we might say, "and we'll do lots of deals with you if this turns out to be a good relationship."

You might pay directly up front for materials needed for a new job, but remember that even when contractors purchase their own materials, they do so on a credit card or an account with the lumber-yard and get thirty-day billing. They don't need money on the spot for the roofing, siding, windows, or anything else for your house. In any event, never pay for the labor until you know that you are happy with the quality of the work. It's seldom in this business that anyone is willing to pay in advance. It's perfectly clear how business should be done.

Nor would I personally advance money to people who are selling properties. As my partner learned when he gave a couple hundred dollars to a man claiming he had a building lot to sell, you can get burned that way. Always use an attorney. Recently, I was getting ready to close on a property in Bay Shore, New York, in a deal that we negotiated over the phone with the sellers. The mother had left an estate, and the heirs wanted to sell it. We came to a price of $182,500. I then said, "Please give me your attorney's contact information, and I will have Lance contact him," which they did.

If those sellers instead had told me: "Let's just write it up ourselves, and you can give us a check for $10,000, just to secure your interest," I would have refused. Who knows? Would I be assured of the chain of title? Would I have known if they had the ability to sell it directly or not, or whether it was still tied up in an estate? Strange things can happen. People even try to sell a property that isn't theirs. There may be liens or judgments on the property.

I'm not sending people a direct check. I'm not signing a contract personally between us. We happen to be in a state where attorneys handle closings. In some states, the title company handles the closings, but I would encourage you to use an attorney almost anywhere. I feel much more confident knowing that he has reviewed the contract and terms of sale. He keeps it all perfectly clear. If you use an attorney, you protect yourself from troubles—including dishonest people.

Trust your gut if you feel you should stay away from somebody. Your instinct should kick right in if someone says: "I'll sell you my house, but you have to sign today and give me just $1,000." Don't do it. It may or may not make sense to offer fifty bucks or so on good faith if you think it helps to seal a deal and you are in a state where attorneys aren't required. But otherwise, no money is to change hands. Instead you make a verbal offer that gets squared away once the contracts are done.

There are a lot of Wimpys out there who want their hamburger today. But payment should come in the right place and time, and they can wait.

TEARS IN HIS EYES

I'm an REO broker, and I list and sell bank-owned properties. I list properties for Fannie Mae, FDIC, Bank of America and Chase, some of the largest banks in the country. I am listing their properties that have been taken back; that is, properties that have come to auction, not been bid on, and reverted to the lender. Occasionally, I will purchase REO properties at good prices, although they sometimes come with headaches.

Once I actually was accused of burglary. As an REO broker, I was representing an out-of-state bank on a property. The bank was taking back the deed in lieu of foreclosure. The owner had bought a two-family house in Queens, set it up as a rental property, and put tenants in, but they immediately began to default. They didn't pay rent for two years, so he was unable to pay the bank. The bank was in the foreclosure process. The owner was one of the nicest guys you'd ever meet, and he was devastated. He lost his down payment and destroyed his credit. He really thought he had a good plan of buying and holding real estate, and it just didn't work.

On the day I met the owner, I was presenting him with a check for $5,000 so the bank wouldn't have to go through the whole foreclosure process. He would deed the house back to the lender. It's called a deed in lieu of foreclosure. In a judicial state like New York, instead of spending two years in the court systems, you can sometimes give the bank the deed to the house. In this particular case, the lender gave him $5,000 to do that.

In my job as the REO broker, I was to meet the owner, James, at the house and give him his $5,000 check. James then fumbled for his keys to begin walking me through three apartments in the building. We had been told that the basement and first floor were vacant, and the second floor was occupied by troublesome tenants. He showed me the basement, and then began to open the door to the first floor.

A woman stuck her head out a first-floor window.

"James. Is that you, James?" she said.

"Latisha, what are you doing in my house?" James asked her. "The sheriff evicted you." She hadn't paid rent for the basement apartment for eighteen months and had been evicted, yet she decided it would be a good idea to reoccupy the house by taking over the first floor.

That's when a second-floor window opened, and people were yelling out that we were breaking in and they were calling the police.

The police came screaming up, an anti-crime team of four plain-clothes guys wearing sweatshirts. "What's going on? We have a report of a burglary," one of them said.

I'm in business attire, standing with the property owner. "My name is Paul Davey. I'm a real estate broker, and I'm here to get the deed from this gentleman and introduce myself to any tenants." I pointed to the second floor. "And that would be those folks who were screaming out that window."

The cops laughed. They were all too familiar with this address—there had been calls before. The tenants were known to be hostile, and the cops invited me to stop by the precinct and they would accompany me if I needed to come back again.

Obviously it was no burglary despite the accusations of the upstairs tenants. The bank wanted those people out. The bank offered the upstairs tenants $32,000 in a "cash for keys" payoff, the biggest settlement that I have ever offered on behalf of a lender. The first-floor tenant was offered $10,000 to just get out. Both rejected the offer. The upstairs apartment rented for $2,000 a month, and they wound up staying two more years. They got $48,000 worth of free rent because of how long it took the bank to get through the eviction process. Finally, the sheriff physically removed them, and I returned with a locksmith.

Ultimately, we sold the property for the bank—but the lender endured quite a hassle. The court also ordered the lender to pay six months' of utilities for both the upstairs and downstairs apartments. The deadbeats took the bank to landlord-tenant court and got their utilities free from November until April, by court mandate. The bank hadn't even had a relationship with those people, and they had cheated the previous owner for two years before the bank took the property back. That's how bad it can get, and in New York City it can get far worse. I wouldn't consider a rental property in the five boroughs.

After I gave James the $5,000 check from the bank for the deed to his property, he told me that this house was supposed to have funded his retirement. He had saved for years to make a down payment for the purchase. It was going to bring in $2,000 a month positive cash flow.

Unfortunately things didn't go quite as planned. He didn't collect the money, the tenants did not pay, and he wound up in foreclosure on the property. All of his investment was lost. He walked away with damaged credit and a small check from the bank. He was devastated. It was a shame to see such a great guy left with tears in his eyes.

CHAPTER 8

Motorcycle in the Living Room

The woman in biker garb appeared at the screen door and squinted out at me. "Yeah, what do you want?" she said, as her four long-haired compatriots, all in leather jackets with Hell's Angels patches, stared at me from their perches on the porch, sipping their beers.

This was back when I had joined with Mark and Rich in starting to buy a lot of foreclosure auction properties. On that particular day in 1997, there were several auctions in the towns of Brookhaven, Babylon, and Islip. So as not to miss any opportunities, we had split up that morning and each had gone to a separate auction, but Rich was the only one of us to successfully bid on a property.

We decided to drive past the house that day in Centereach, a working class town. We usually did that after buying a house. Sometimes the owner still occupies the house and you can get a conversation started about their relocation plans.

At the time, I was still working construction jobs, and I was driving my beat-up pickup truck, a Ford 250 with 265,000 miles. I was looking pretty beat up myself, still in my work clothes.

I met my partners a block away from the house. They were driving a $130,000 Mercedes and dressed in nice suits—you could say they were in a different spot than I was at the time. We cruised past the house and saw motorcycles parked around it and the four men hanging out on the front porch. So we pulled down the block and I got out to talk with my partners about the situation.

"Listen, let me go up to the house and introduce myself," I told them as they sat in the Mercedes, "and see if I can get a little dialogue going. You guys might not do well here."

I got back in my pickup, pulled up to the house, and walked to the porch.

"How are you doing?" I asked as politely as I could manage. "Owner around?" One of the men called through the screen door for the woman, who seemed to be the boss. As she sized me up through the screen, I could see into the living room—and couldn't help but to notice a motorcycle parked inside.

The woman squinted at me. "Yeah, what do you want?" she asked.

"I work for some guys who think they bought this house at an auction this morning," I told her. "And I wanted to come by and introduce myself."

She peered at me and cursed. "It was f—ing canceled," she said. "Didn't happen. You can call my lawyer."

"Okay, cool, must be a mistake—thanks, sorry for the inconvenience," I said, and headed back to my truck.

I figured she was in denial, with her Hell's Angels pals to back her up, so I drove down the block to meet up with Mark and Rich.

"She says it wasn't sold," I told them. Rich looked puzzled. We called the law firm handling the foreclosure auction and confirmed that the sale had indeed been postponed. Rich was starting to look a little ashen. We pulled out the foreclosure list and studied it. Sure enough, the house he had bought at auction that morning was on that street—but it was five blocks away.

At least the correct house was vacant. We weren't going to be dealing with any Hell's Angels. But Rich hadn't bought the house he thought he was buying. He'd made a mistake in his bidding that easily could have cost us money.

RISKY BUSINESS

Auction purchases are the riskiest of all distressed real estate transactions. To give you some perspective on why inexperienced buyers should avoid them, let me explain how an experienced buyer handles auction purchases.

First, we will have done our due diligence on a computer and pulled up our numbers and have a good idea of what the house would be worth once renovated. We look at the property as closely as possible, depending on whether it is vacant. We walk the property, get inside if we can, check out the basement, take some notes, and come up with a price to renovate it. I use my pricing guide for that. I plug numbers in, including the fact that I want a profit of 17 to 20 percent. That tells me how much I can bid for the property at auction.

That's my price point. Then I get to the auction a few minutes early and double-check the Long Island Profiles to make sure I'm looking at the right property.

> **You must know your price point, and if the bidding exceeds that amount, consider yourself out. It's a math formula, so don't let emotion cloud your judgment.**

New York is a judicial state, so unlike in some other states, fore-closures go through the courts. After the courts approve the sale, an appointee (known here as the referee) puts the property up for auction on the designated day, announcing the minimum bid. On the fore-closure auction list, we can see the amount of the final judgment—let's say that it was $379,000. From that, we can assume that the bank's minimum price, the upset price, also will be about $379,000. That indeed might be where the bidding kicks off, although with the recent glut of foreclosures it could open for $70,000 or $80,000 less than that.

If nobody bids, the property reverts to the lender at the upset price. However, if there is some equity and bidders can see that the property is worth more, several investors are likely to start bidding up the price, sometimes in increments of $500. The referee may call for $1,000 increments.

If you are among those bidders, you must know your price point, and if the bidding exceeds that amount, consider yourself out. I can't emphasize that enough: It's a math formula, and don't let emotion cloud your judgment. People get caught up in the emotion and the excitement, as if they were gambling in Atlantic City or Las Vegas. They want to win—but winning isn't the goal. The goal is to make money in real estate safely and consistently.

Sometimes, when new people get caught in the excitement, some of the experienced investors will keep bidding them up. If that happens to you, you will pay considerably more than you planned to pay and should pay. If you see other bidders getting excited and boosting the price, and you get caught up in that, it will cost you money.

Foreclosure auctions are interesting to see, and I certainly would recommend that a new investor go to one to see how they work in action. Just be cautious about getting involved right away. A lot of times, the auctions will be posted in the county courthouses if you don't want to subscribe to a full foreclosure list. You can come across some good leads there.

DON'T GO HOME IN HANDCUFFS

If you attend enough foreclosure auctions, you will notice a core group of people who go there all the time. New people come and go, and some people may buy one house and then you don't see them for six or eight months. In good times, there certainly are deals to be had at the auction. But some guys who haunt these auctions try to make those deals even better.

Let's say the minimum bid is $150,000. A few bidders might collude. "Tommy, look, it doesn't make sense for you to bid this place up to $200,000 to get it," Bob whispers to him. "The bank just wants the upset price. So let's do this instead: You let me have this one. If you don't bid against me this morning, I won't bid against you this afternoon on the house I know you really have your eye on."

That's one way they'll do it. Another trick is to collude for somebody to buy the house at a dollar over the minimum—say, $150,001. Then Bob, Tommy, Frank and Steve will go to a diner and hold their own silent auction. If Bob bids the most, perhaps $160,000, he will get the referee's deed, and he gives the others $2,500 apiece. That puts the money that would have gone to the bank into their own pockets. They divvy up the spoils.

However the mechanics of it work, it's all illegal. It's collusion. You can be arrested for racketeering. Do an online search for collusion arrests at foreclosure auctions, and you will see that people get caught for it regularly. The authorities sometimes send in somebody who pretends to be a bidder. Sometimes one of the colluders will be arrested for a different offense and start talking.

Do it the right way. If you decide to buy at auctions, don't accept money not to bid. Don't agree to hold off bidding at 10 o'clock if someone promises not to bid at 1 o'clock. The temptation can be attractive—if you have a criminal mindset. But even those who are fundamentally honest have been led astray by the lure of a quick buck.

> **Do an online search for collusion arrests at fore-closure auctions, and you will see that people get caught for it regularly.**

If you're going into this business, you probably will want to keep it up a long time. You should want that consistent 17 to 20 percent return on your investment, doubling your money every four or five years. You should want to honestly grow a nice nest egg for your retirement and to help your family. The moment the handcuffs snap around your wrists, you will have lost that dream.

Somebody arrested for mortgage fraud or other dirty dealings might try to report all the others with whom he has been running scams for years. In a desperate attempt to save his own neck, he pretends that he is still part of the clique. Bob, Tommy, Frank and Steve head out to the diner for their deal—but this time, Bob is wearing a government wire and records their private little auction.

The point is that you must do business honestly and ethically. Don't look for quick fixes in life, and don't look for free money. It's not free. It has a big price tag at the end—so stay away from the crooks. They'll tempt you to save $10,000, and you'll end up with a racketeering charge—and there goes your career. You can make plenty while still playing by the rules.

The criminals usually wind up in prison, but there are plenty of scammers out there. They will know that you are ambitious and that you want to make big bucks. The desire to get ahead is honorable, so never let anyone pervert it. Don't look for quick fixes. You need to do some work and put your time in and figure things out. You're writing a success story, not a crime story.

A WORD ON REOS

Lately, a lot of houses have reverted to the lender at foreclosure auctions and become REOs. I think these are a much better option than buying at auction. You are able to get into those properties and inspect them. You can examine them in as much detail as you want. You can even bring in your subcontractors, because they are vacant houses. You can make an appointment with the REO broker or your own broker and spend some time looking at it. You're not going to be involved with an eviction.

In addition, foreclosed property may have title issues that can delay the sale. If you're buying at an auction, you want to be buying the first position mortgage, which would knock out second mortgages, equity lines, and just about everything other than a tax lien, but it's somewhat complicated. However, if you're buying an REO property, the bank has to clear all those title issues up before it can sell the property to you. The burden is really on the bank. You're not under the pressure of an auction purchase where you are expected to close in 30 days. Remember: You could forfeit a deposit if you're unable to close.

I've had success throughout the fifteen years that I've been investing in real estate because we often buy regular properties, many off the multiple listing, that need renovation or expansion. We'll buy Ranches and Capes and turn them into Colonials. Almost on a weekly basis, there's a property that I can buy for $225,000, put $100,000 into it, and then sell it in the low-fours. Those deals are available if you embrace the rehabbing end. You don't need to buy foreclosures or REOs to be successful.

Don't buy occupied houses, especially not in the beginning. If you're buying in a liberal place like New York City, make sure you're familiar with the municipal policies and make sure you can deal with them. Would it be okay with you to hold on to a property for an 18-month eviction and possibly be ordered to pay the utilities for people who never paid their rent and whom you didn't put there to begin with? If you're okay with all that, go for it—but count me out.

CHAPTER 9

40 Projects to Sandy Lane

There is a book that I like called *The Compound Effect,* by Darren Hardy. He is the publisher of *SUCCESS* Magazine. I also listen to the audio program regularly in my car. One of his lines, in quotes, that really hit me is, "The Compound Effect is the principle of reaping huge rewards from a series of small, smart choices.... Even though the results are massive, the steps, in the moment, don't seem significant."

If you take small steps every day, the effects over a three to five year period can be profound. Hardy offers an example that goes something like this: You want to lose 30 pounds, so you eat sensibly for a week, stop drinking, and exercise. At the end of the week, you get on the scale and you have lost one or two pounds. "Screw this," you might say—but a couple of hundred fewer calories a day could mean that you would reach your goal in a year.

We want instant gratification. We want results tomorrow, but there is a tremendous compound effect of making small, smart choices and repeating them over and over. That's how it went for me: slowly. When I was working as a cop in the 40 Projects, I was making only about $8 an hour in take-home pay in one of the most violent places in the city. The violence and problems there were devastating.

Through good luck, hard work, and a series of simple steps, however, I moved in the right direction. I now make more than 25 times my starting police salary. Real estate has been the main vehicle that has helped me get there. Construction has played a role in it. It has been a compound effect of slow and steady progress in a direction that I wanted to go.

We recently traveled to Sandy Lane in Barbados, an incredible place to take a vacation. I don't say that to brag; I just want to illustrate the possibilities to which you, too, can aspire. No rich uncle died. I did not become a brain surgeon. I am a high school graduate. Instead I learned a business. I took some simple, proven steps and repeated them systematically, while dealing along the way with the kind of problems that everybody has.

We also understand the importance of giving back. You may not have much money when you get started in this business. But as your success builds, you should give a percentage of what you make to religious or charitable institutions that are important to you. We are major supporters of the St. Francis Breadline in the city that feeds the hungry and the homeless, and of the Wounded Warrior project that supports men and women who are fighting for our safety around the world.

It's not about the mere pursuit of money. It's about what money can do for the betterment of ourselves and our families and our communities. You can't say the pursuit of wealth is evil if you consider the extent to which generous giving has helped people. Money opens doors of opportunity. I was a good guy in my early 20s. I just didn't have any really good ideas. I wasn't aware of the truth of the

Compound Effect and how small steps, one after the next, lead to a great destination. It took a long time for me to see that.

Money enhances your lifestyle and your comforts, yes, but it also allows you to reach out to others. If you are only making money for yourself, your wealth will feel shallow. You are likely to try harder and go further if you have a bigger "why" behind your wealth, whether providing your children a good education or helping people in need.

I love this business. I like to see the transformation from a distressed property to a beautifully renovated property. I love the compliments that we get when I am at a closing table. That's deeply gratifying. We are selling used houses, and though there's no warranty, I stand behind the workmanship of those who do my renovations. If you buy one of our houses and six months later there is a leaky pipe in the bathroom, we will send the plumber to take care of it. Few sellers do that, but we aim to serve.

Not only can you help others in this business, but you need to accept help from others. You need to recognize where you need help. You can do this. You just have to be willing to take good advice, use your brain, be reasonable, be sensible, and play by the rules. It may seem a long way from the 40 Projects to Sandy Lane, but if you are like me, once you get started you will find the journey fascinating and fulfilling.

What Hump?

I f you've never seen the Mel Brooks classic "Young Franken-stein," put down my book, fire up your Blu-ray, and enjoy. I particularly like the scene in which Gene Wilder, as the misguided doctor, offers to remove the huge shoulder hump of his misshapen assistant, Igor, played by Marty Feldman:

Dr. Frankenstein: "You know, I'm a rather brilliant surgeon. Perhaps I can help you with that hump."

Igor: What hump?

True, Igor's hump kept shifting from one shoulder to the other, but it should have been quite apparent even to his bug eyes. He didn't see the obvious flaw that nobody else could miss.

We all have humps, whether we recognize them or not. What is yours—and can anyone help you with it? Do you know what is holding you back? You may dream of a life as a highly paid real estate investor, broker or contractor, but you're stuck in a 9-to-5 dead-end job that doesn't feed those ambitions. You just can't seem to get over that hump.

If that describes you, rest assured that there are people who have the information that you need. I did not realize this. I got a little smarter as I got older. I began to read a lot. Today I read at least a book a week and listen to educational CDs all the time. Pretty much all the information in the world is available at public libraries.

If you are interested in wealth building or dealing in distressed real estate, you will find no shortage of information on that subject. If you want to make money, a wealth of knowledge awaits you. You just need to avail yourself of it, whether by diving into a book, listening to a tape, joining a club, or paying attention to a mentor who taps you on the shoulder and says, "I can help you." If something inside you has been saying, "I want to be more, and learn more," then it's time to answer that call.

A lot of people in this world are oblivious to their humps. Perhaps it's a drinking problem that gets in the way of growth and ambition until nothing but the bottle matters. The first step to recovery is recognizing that. Or perhaps the self-defeating attitude of "I can't do it" is so deeply ingrained in you that your efforts are doomed before they begin, because they never do begin. We all have different humps. A lot of us, like Igor, just can't see how much better life could be.

In *The Brower Quadrant*, Lee Brower emphasizes the importance of "contribution" as one of four crucial arenas for one's assets. He tells of a woman with cancer who had asked to talk to him. He called her and she proceeded to tell him about her illness, the treatment and medications, and all the details about her condition. He listened politely and quietly and decided that she needed a paradigm shift.

"I understand your problems," he told her, "but what are you doing for other people right now? How are you being of service to others?" That is this man's governing principle: service to others. We all know people with an illness whose lives have seemed consumed by it. It's all they talk about. They don't look for the positives. But if you only focus on your illness, or on your problem, you are in a very dark corner.

It's a good question to ask yourself, whatever your endeavor: How are you being of service to others? Are you giving of yourself, whether it's money or time? As soon as you begin doing so, the world opens up to you, your mind opens up, and you are not so intensely focused on the negative.

I was in that dark place back when I stood in the rain in the 40 Projects, before I saw a brighter path. In this book, I have explained how I found a route to wealth through real estate, particularly distressed properties. If you want to go that way, I'm happy to help. But whatever your endeavor, be sure to both reach up and reach out.

By bettering yourself, you are increasingly able to serve others. By serving others, you are bettering yourself. Take a look at your shoulder and see whether there's a hump to remove, and head on out to experience the unencumbered life.

"An aim in life
is the only fortune worth finding;
and it is not to be found in foreign lands,
but in the heart itself."

-Robert Louis Stevenson

Sample Investor Cover Letter

I have used the following letter to investors to raise several million dollars from friends, family members and accredited investors. My investor partners have been able to safely generate 10 to 12 percent returns, and I have been able to greatly expand my distressed real estate investing business.

Please feel free to use this letter as a template to assist you in creating your own investor letter. For most of us, private capital is the lifeblood of this business, and I have included this as free bonus for my readers because I know that the lack of capital is what held me back. I'm giving you the blueprint to raise money—now it's up to you!

Sincerely,
Paul Davey

Dear _____,

As soon as I had a moment to read the just-released *Forbes' 2012 Investment Guide,* I thought of you.

I couldn't wait to sit right down and invite you to become one of my private real estate investor partners. Investing in the rehabilitation of distressed real estate is what *Forbes, Money Magazine* (and many other retirement experts) recommend for today's smart investors. And that is you—a smart investor. And that is me—a distressed property rehab investor and specialist.

But like *Forbes* also recommends, you <u>must</u> ensure you find someone you can trust to help you with these types of investments. Someone who knows what they're doing—and is on the up-and-up. You've known me for years as a loyal friend and trustworthy person. I can tell you that *my personal retirement account is up 23% YTD thanks to my real estate rehab investments. And all of my private investor partners' accounts are up 10-12%.*

So what makes this investment option more viable, more secure and more stable than the other hundreds of options you are most likely bombarded with each year?

Here's the deal: You know me well enough to know that I'm not some fly-by-night businessman. If I come to you with an opportunity to make a <u>solid</u> 10% return on investment in passive income with <u>full</u> security, you can be assured that is PRECISELY what it will be.

And you and I have both been around long enough to hear about all of the "passive income opportunities" out there today. Let's be honest, the majority of those "opportunities" are neither "passive" nor "opportunities." We've probably all been sucked into one or another over the years. But I assure you—this is NOT one of those.

My 20-year career as a well-respected New York City police sergeant speaks to my honesty and integrity. And my 25 years specializing in the purchase, renovation and re-sale of single family homes— *having completed over $19,000,000 worth of rehab projects resulting in profits of more than $4,000,000 for myself and my partners*—speaks to the success and security of this viable investment option.

You know I'm a plain-talker. So, let's get down to it. Rather than continuing to waste time with bank CDs that offer 1% returns, or volatile and uncertain money market accounts or mutual funds…

…investing in distressed real estate using CASH accounts or within SELF DIRECTED IRAs is what investment

"I have been investing in my brother Paul's real estate deals since the late 1990s with cash accounts and, more recently, with my self-directed IRA funds. He offers a great way to quickly and safely grow your money. In the years to come, my position as 'Being the Bank' will lead to an annual six-figure income for me!"

—Phil Davey, Captain
NYC Fire Dept., Retired

experts (as in the 2012 *Forbes' Investment Guide*) strongly recommend in today's investment climate.

As I mentioned in my *"Rehab and Grow Rich"* chapter of the Amazon best-selling book, **Gamechangers**, my private investor partners are delighted with the returns they're getting, both in cash and in their retirement accounts—some doubling their accounts safely in as little as seven years.

The money invested grows securely and solidly without their time commitment or involvement. They don't have to know how to do it. I do it for them. And because I've been a general contractor since 1987, buying real estate since 1992 and have made $4 million in profits for myself and my partners, I have a firm foundation to stand on.

I know, first-hand, that this is solid and trustworthy. And I know, first-hand that it works. I wouldn't invest with my own self-directed IRAs and cash accounts if I didn't know that for a fact.

In more than $19,000,000 worth of distressed real estate transactions completed over the years, I've never had a losing deal; and no investor has ever failed to receive his or her principal investment plus 10-12% interest. Really.

So, whatever has been keeping you up at night, whether it's funding one of your child's or grandchild's college educations, uncertainty about your secure and comfortable retirement accounts, fear of outliving your money, or if you just want an additional stream of income...**imagine growing your personal retirement account 10-12% annually through investing in our real estate rehab projects.**

HERE'S JUST ONE SUCCESS STORY (OF THE LITERALLY HUNDREDS I COULD GIVE YOU FROM OVER THE YEARS):

My investment company and my IRA purchased a fire damaged property as "Tenants in Common," each with a 50% undivided interest. Purchase price was $184,000.

{BEFORE}

The property required a $120,000 renovation—and those costs were also split equally by my investment company and my IRA ($60,000 each).

After renovations, the property sold for $457,000—resulting in a net profit, after all the expenses, of $137,000. $68,500 profit was returned to my IRA, 100% tax deferred, and $68,500 profit went to my investment company (as taxable income).

{AFTER}

> **The final result?**
> A 43% return on investment.
>
> **Total time from initial purchase to completed renovation and resale?** 7 months.
>
> **Annual ROI?** Approximately 72%.

Did you know that there are currently hundreds of properties in our local market ready to be purchased at significant discounts to their after repaired value? I am offering select family and friends, like you, an opportunity to enjoy 10-12% rates of return with minimum or no risk. Smart investors have been utilizing this investment vehicle for years—it is a very safe investment strategy that provides both a high rate-of-return and security.

Banks and lending institutions need to liquidate their inventory in order to reduce their liability and increase lending capacity. So,

*What is a Private Loan?

A private loan is a loan made to a real estate investor that is secured by real estate. Private Loan Investors are given a first or second mortgage that secures their legal interest in the property and secures their investment. We are not talking about high loan-to-value (LTV) ratios that banks were previously making on homes.

as investors, we are now purchasing properties for pennies of what they were last sold for…usually 60-70 cents on the dollar!

HERE IS HOW OUR FINELY-TUNED INVESTMENT PROCESS WORKS:

#1—The Product:

We buy our product (i.e. distressed single family homes) at 60-70 cents on the dollar through private loans*. These properties are bank owned, estate sales, handyman specials, fire/structurally damaged and expansion opportunities (turning Capes into Colonials…see Sugar Maple property example.)

Our repeatable model provides us with access to a steady flow of investment opportunities at 60-70% of their after repaired value (ARV).

Sugar Maple (Before)

Purchase Price: $188,000

Sugar Maple (After)

#2—The Work:

As a real estate broker who specializes in REO or bank-owned properties, my current clients include: Fannie Mae, Chase, Bank of America, FDIC and Astoria Federal Savings. I also have a network of brokers in this specialized field with access to a large number of investment opportunities on an ongoing basis. I tell you that not to brag, but to assure you that I know what I'm doing and am in-the-know with this niche market.

Now, this next part is the key to our longevity and success—and to your investment…

We have been licensed general contractors and builders since 1987 (www.SligoConstruction.com). From the beginning, our rehab projects have been completed in-house to ensure wholesale pricing and the quickest turn-around times in the industry.

That makes ALL the difference. When I'm involved in the PURCHASE, the REHAB, and the SALE of these properties…nothing gets by me. Ever.

#3—The Investment Rewards & Assurance:

Tax-Deferred Growth Opportunity—Your money can grow at 10-12% annually. And it is fully-collateralized by real estate, so you can invest with confidence. This is IRA-suitable…your money can compound, tax-deferred until age 70 ½ or until you start withdrawals.

Sold: $385,000
Net Profit: $66,000
ROI: 22.85%.

Passive Income—Earn 10-12% passive income while you continue working in your profession or as a supplement to your retirement income.

Invest with Confidence—I have been investing in distressed real estate with my own cash and IRA funds for many years (since 1992). In $19,000,000+ worth of transactions, we have never had a losing deal and no investor has failed to receive their principal investment, plus 10-12% interest.

Invest with an Advantage—I like to invest in places where I have an advantage. I am not a stock market investor (no advantage for me). However, as a real estate investor I have powerful advantages that feed the growth of your investment.

Real Estate Broker—Because I specialize in REO (bank owned) properties, HUD & auction properties, I have access to all the up-to-the-minute data (i.e. Multiple Listing Service, market-by-market sales activity, foreclosure and Lis Pendis lists, Estate Sales, Handyman Specials, expireds, etc.)

General Contractor/Builder—My in-house crews provide rapid turn-around and wholesale construction pricing. I have a long history of successful deals which insures accurate cost estimates and project time lines.

Full-Time Investor—I am in the market every day, evaluating deals and looking for the best current opportunities for capital allocation. I have a network of REALTORS®, attorneys, wholesalers, insurance adjusters and mortgage brokers that refer business to me on an ongoing basis because we close quickly and in cash.

Because I've been doing this for so long, you can see I've thought of everything. Every detail is covered, every logistical aspect— handled. This is a business. And I treat it as such. And I want you, your family and your retirement account to reap the rewards from this business along with me and mine.

Here is a deal that recently closed. The reward for my private investor is a safe 10% return when his bank was offering 2% rate on a 3-year CD!

GARDINERS AVENUE

{BEFORE}

Purchase price: $178,000

Repairs: $53,000

Carrying costs: $11,000

Commission: $7,500

Total Costs (from above): $249,500

{AFTER}

Sales price: $305,000

ROI: 21%

Time in deal: 9 months

I could give you 100 more examples like this, but I think you get the point by now.

A few questions may have come to mind as you've been reading this letter. That's great...I'm a question guy myself. Because of that, I've included a few common FAQs at the end of this letter.

If you have more questions or simply want to have a discussion, give me a call on my personal cell: xxx-xxx-xxxx or e-mail me: **Paul@ RehabandGrowRich.com**

If you're ready to gain a secure, passive income of 10-12% right now, then let me know. We are bursting with investment properties just waiting for you. This is solid and trustworthy. And smart.

Remember, e-mail me at: **Paul@RehabandGrowRich.com**

If you're not quite ready to move forward but would like more information on investing in real estate using your self-directed IRA, that is great! Just let me know, and I'll send you my free report entitled, *The Seven Steps to IRA Riches*. It's full of valuable no-obligation information.

Thanks for your time and interest.

All the best to you and your family,
Paul Davey
Paul@RehabandGrowRich.com

How do I invest tax-free?

A Self-Directed IRA is legally no different from any other IRA. It allows you, the client, to choose your IRA investments. Giving you the option to invest in a wide range of opportunities—with some exceptions listed below.

[The only assets excluded by the IRS are life insurance contracts, collectibles, and capital stock in an "S" Corporation. You can verify that it's legal to invest your IRA in mortgage notes by going to the IRS website and researching what cannot be held in an IRA.]

Is this new?

No. You've been able to buy real estate and mortgage notes within your IRA since IRAs were created over 30 years ago. Many financial professionals are unfamiliar with this and continue to recommend Stocks, Bonds and Mutual Funds for IRA investments. Some institutions limit investment choices to funds and products for which they'll earn a commission.

How do I use my IRA or pension plan?

Making real estate loans is a widely accepted use for IRAs and other Retirement Plans. Most people do not know that you can make private mortgage loans using the funds which are already in your

IRAs and other retirement plans. Think of the power of loaning out funds at high interest rates that are tax-free or tax-deferred!

In order for you to use retirement accounts for loans they must first be administered by a third-party custodian. One custodian we commonly work with is Equity Trust Company. You can visit them on the web at www.trustetc.com or simply talk to us and we'll help you with the set up of your account.

After selecting your custodian, you simply send a transfer form to them and they'll do all of the work for you. Once you've done that you are ready to make private mortgage loans.

From there you simply notify your custodian about the investment you are looking to make and they will send the check for the gross amount of the loan. *Even better, we can do all the work for you. You just sign a few docs, sit back, relax and wait for your money to grow tax-free or deferred.*

What's the minimum investment?

The minimum investment is $200,000 individually or collectively as an entity.

Who handles all of the details?

We do. It's our job to get you proper documentation and protect your interest. All of this costs you nothing. We pay all costs. If you make a $200,000 loan, you send a check for $200,000 to our closing attorney and you get a mortgage for $200,000.

How do I get paid?

The majority of our investors receive a one-time principle plus interest payment after the completion and sale of a project. For accounting reasons, this is a preferred way for our company as well.

Is this a long-term investment?

Our projects are short-term renovation and re-sales. Loan terms are typically 12-24 months. When long term buy and hold properties are considered we would offer longer loan terms.

What if I need to liquidate?

If you want out, a 60-day written notice is required, because we will need to replace your funds with another investor's money. You really shouldn't make mortgage loans if you feel you will liquidate this shortly, but the option is always available, and we have been able to liquidate in as little as two weeks in some scenarios.

Is my investment really as safe as it sounds?

Yes! We always follow these common sense guidelines that we've talked about. Your money can grow two, three, or even four times faster than your current investments—and you maintain control.

Each one of our properties that we acquire is put through a rigorous financial evaluation in order to determine the profitability before the property is ever purchased.

Can I get updates on the progress of the property I hold a mortgage on?

You will receive a quarterly report with photos and current status of project.

Do I receive title insurance?

Yes. Title insurance is provided by a national title company.

How is the property insured?

Through traditional homeowner's insurance or a builder's risk policy for large renovation projects naming the mortgage holder as additional insured.

Purchase Criteria / Property Selection

We primarily purchase 3 types of properties:

1. Distressed properties to be renovated as they currently exist.

2. Expansion opportunities—properties that can be turned from a ranch or cape into a colonial.

3. Fire and structurally damaged properties requiring major renovations

What interest rate will I be paid?

First position mortgages receive 10% interest paid at the time of the property re-sale.

Can I get a higher rate of interest?

Second position mortgages may be utilized to fund rehab costs and these mortgages will pay 12% interest.

How do you determine the price you will pay for a property?

1. Purchase decisions are based on MLS (Multiple Listing Service) data. Specifically, we look at properties that

have closed in the past 90 days. This shows us what like properties are selling for today.

2. Our proprietary construction cost estimating system gives us repair costs.

3. We calculate our holding costs (attorney, title, insurance, taxes, utilities, real estate commissions, etc.).

4. We add our projected repair costs and holding costs and subtract them from what the MLS has told us the property should sell for based on recent sales data. We then multiply that number by 17%- 20% profit goal. This gives us the target purchase price for each property we submit an offer on.

Actual example—Gardiners Avenue (pg.4-5)

- Estimated after repaired value (ARV) per MLS comps: $295,000

- Construction cost estimator repair cost estimate: $55,000

- Total holding costs estimate: $16,000

- Target profit: $44,000

- Target purchase price: $178,000

We were able to purchase this property for our target price of $178,000. Our construction costs were $2,000 less than our system estimated and our holding costs were $2,500 more than planned. Property sold in 3 days for $305,000 which was $10,000 more than our target sale price.

My private investor partner was paid 10% interest on a first mortgage of $178,000 (approximately 61% loan to ARV). My investment company paid for the renovation and holding costs.

RECOMMENDED READING

1. *The Magic of Thinking Big*—David Schwartz

2. *The Compound Effect*—Darren Hardy

3. *IRA Wealth: Revolutionary IRA Strategies for Real Estate Investment*—Patrick W. Rice

4. *No B.S. Ruthless Management of People and Profits*—Dan Kennedy

5. *The Brower Quadrant*—Lee Brower

6. *Real Wealth by Investing in Real Estate*—Ralph Roberts

7. *Think and Grow Rich*—Napoleon Hill

8. *Winning Through Intimidation*—Robert J. Ringer

9. *Work the System*—Sam Carpenter

10. *The Ultimate Sales Machine*—Chet Holmes

How can you use this book?

MOTIVATE

EDUCATE

THANK

INSPIRE

PROMOTE

CONNECT

Why have a custom version of *Rehab & Grow Rich?*

- Build personal bonds with customers, prospects, employees, donors, and key constituencies
- Develop a long-lasting reminder of your event, milestone, or celebration
- Provide a keepsake that inspires change in behavior and change in lives
- Deliver the ultimate "thank you" gift that remains on coffee tables and bookshelves
- Generate the "wow" factor

Books are thoughtful gifts that provide a genuine sentiment that other promotional items cannot express. They promote employee discussions and interaction, reinforce an event's meaning or location, and they make a lasting impression. Use your book to say "Thank You" and show people that you care.

Rehab and Grow Rich is available in bulk quantities and in customized versions at special discounts for corporate, institutional, and educational purposes. To learn more please contact our Special Sales team at:

1.866.775.1696 • sales@advantageww.com • www.AdvantageSpecialSales.com

CPSIA information can be obtained at www.ICGtesting.com
Printed in the USA
BVOW04s0954311013

335148BV00013B/271/P